THE GIRL WITH THE CATERPILLAR EYEBROWS

Survival. Resilience. Triumph.

by Lisa Ditchkoff

To Rick,
Thank you ♡
looking forward!
Lisa Ditchkoff

DEDICATION

To my sons: Zack and Trey.

If I had a list of character traits I could pass on to you, resiliency would be on top, along with a good work ethic, a survivor mentality, and a heart to make the world a better place. May you learn from my life.

TABLE OF CONTENTS

TABLE OF CONTENTS CONTINUED

FOREWORD

Lisa's story has all the ingredients that will keep the reader enthralled: heartache, disappointment, suffering, and yet, time and again, it shows the power of the human spirit to prevail. I found her story unique in that she remains objective and treats every player in her saga with respect, whether deserved or not.

Why should you read this book? There are the usual reasons—to gain inspiration from her infinite capacity to persevere, to identify with her mistakes, some of which most of us have made ourselves, and to experience along with Lisa the joy she feels as her three decade time of involuntary hiding finally ends in restored family relationships. But for me the reason is deeper. As the story evolves we discover a woman of substance who had to gain that backbone on her own with precious few mentors along the way— a former customer of Lisa's when she was a waitress in a pizza parlor as a teenager was a notable exception.

Lisa is a modern heroine of sorts . . . flawed yet resilient, and thereby heroic. She is amazingly candid and revealing as she shares each vignette. Her style communicates clearly while being sensitive to her characters. She obviously trusts her readers, allowing them into the intimate corners of her heart. Her catharsis of emotions and frustrations left me exhausted but fulfilled. I started reading about an escape, read what seemed to be an infinite number of hurdles in her path, but gradually felt like I was right there with her, determined to finish the race. At thirty-nine, Lisa has lived a lifetime. I have an enriched appreciation of what forges a person of indomitable character and love for others through service. She truly lives in the "selfless zone." She has a soul of steel and heart of service. May her journey enrich you as it has me.

Stretch Dunn
Colonel (USA Ret)
Hoover, Alabama
June 2013

Stretch and Lisa.

"This was on my porch this morning, Judy, and it scares the shit out of me."

My mom's good friend Bridgett handed her a bouquet of black flowers that was wrapped in white butcher paper with a little card attached. There was a huge black satin bow around them.

I couldn't read yet, but I knew the note was short. My mother read it quickly and whispered, "Omigod! Did you see who left these?" Her voice grew louder. "Oh . . . my . . . God!"

"Mommy, can I see?"

"Yeah, Mom, I didn't know there was such a thing as black roses," my brother Scott said.

My mother didn't seem to hear us. "Tim, take these and throw them in the garbage can—now! Shove 'em down inside so no one can see what they are!" My mom yelled to my oldest brother, who had been doing his homework at our kitchen table. She shoved the parcel into his hands.

"Youch, Ma, they have thorns in them!" he protested, but he wasted no time. "What's going on, Ma?"

"Your daddy had someone leave these at Bridgett's."

She handed the card to Tim and he read it loud enough for me to hear. "'Keep Judy away from that biker.' Ma, what does that mean?"

"I don't know, but your father is capable of anything," she answered. "Black roses, death threats, and I hear through the vine that there's a hit out on me. We're not gonna hang around long enough to find out what other surprises he has for us."

INTRODUCTION

"You're so beautiful," my father said, as he picked me up above his head to look at me. I was four years old, and those three words are my only memory of him from my childhood. I imagine that last day with him now, picturing my thick blonde hair blowing softly around my face as the breeze from Boston Harbor tickled my cheeks. He had come by the flat on Peter Street where Mommy, Scotty, Tim, and I lived, and he took my two brothers and me for a walk on Carson Beach. He had a roll of dimes and gave some of them to each of us to buy some candy from the snack bar at Castle Island.

We left Boston in February of the year I was four years old. I knew nothing more of him for nearly thirty years: I didn't know what he looked like, where he lived, if he had gotten married again, or what he did to earn a living. My mother wouldn't talk about him other than to say he was an alleged mobster and a dangerous man, a member of the South Boston Irish Mafia, and we were hiding from him. I remember hearing the name Whitey Bulger.

Memories of my father were shadowy ones, but I remembered him as generous in his love toward me and my brothers. What could be so horrible about him? As I grew older and had children of my own, I wondered about that answer.

Then one day I had the opportunity to find out. I found my father in South Boston, still living only a few miles from where he was born. Having recently spent three years in federal prison, he was trying to live a quiet life under the radar.

I have decided to write this memoir because I believe my story can provide inspiration and hope that some may need to help them believe in themselves enough to achieve a goal or pursue a dream. I've shared parts of my story with individuals and groups and people have said to me, "You should write a book about your life."

I do think I have an unusual story. Though I am only forty years old at the time of this writing, I have two sons, one who is twenty-three and another who is nineteen. I have beaten the odds that predicted my lack of education and single teenage motherhood would slot me into the welfare system. I was so determined to try and give my child(ren) a good life and believed education was key. Though completely illiterate resulting in taking college Comp I three times and Comp II twice, I finally graduated after seven years of persevering. I've undergone sexual, emotional, and physical abuse which nearly took my life.

When someone tells a story, the best way is usually to start at the beginning. So that's what I'll do.

I invite you to come along with me while I take us back to South Boston, Massachusetts, where my story began, to "Southie," where I, like my father, my mother, and two brothers, was born. We'll visit a housing project and some local hangouts. Let's climb up the steps at Dorchester Heights where a monument commemorates George Washington's first victory of the American Revolution. Let's see the skyline of downtown Boston to our left before we climb down "The Golden Steps" to get to the narrow three-story house where my mother grew up. We can stop into a gym or two where young men like my father still punch and pummel each other, training for that big boxing match they hope to participate in. Southie was my mother's and father's world, and it still is my father's. It would have been mine, too, if my mother had not packed up my two brothers and me and secretly left Southie in the middle of the night during the biggest snowstorm in Boston's history in 1978, the storm providing my mother's only window of escape.

THE ESCAPE

"Okay. We'll be ready. No, he doesn't know and if he finds out, there'll be hell to pay. I'm worried someone will tell him, but so far I haven't seen or heard from him for days. We gotta get out of here before he figures out we're going and someone shows up here with a gun."

I heard my mother's voice from the kitchen talking to someone on the phone as I sat on the floor in front of the TV munching on a bowl of dry Cheerios. I didn't know who "he" was, but he sounded mean. I popped the Cheerios into my mouth one by one while I watched Romper Room. Miss Sherry held up her mirror to look in it and I listened for the names of the Good Little Do-Bees.

[We interrupt this program. The city of Boston is continuing its snow emergency regulations. The record snowfall of 27.1 inches has virtually shut down the city. All parked cars must be off major thoroughfares so that snow removal equipment can clear the roads. Mayor Kevin White has asked that all residents stay in their homes and tuned to their TV sets. Thank you.]

That's what we had been doing for the past two days. The boys wanted to take their sleds to Dorchester Heights, but the snow was so heavy and high that we couldn't even open the door.

"Lisa, come here now! Hurry up!" Mommy called me as she stood by the coat rack at the front door. She made me stand still while she forced my arms into my coat.

"Stand still, Lisa! We need to get this on! Scotty, put down the truck and get your jacket on. Tim, help Scotty. We need to hurry!"

"Ma, where we going? How we even gonna get out 'o' the door?" Nine-year-old Tim tried to push it open, but the snowdrift on the front porch was taller than he was.

"Ma, maybe we could dig a tunnel!" Scotty sounded excited.

My mother handed a box to Tim and a suitcase to Scotty. "Get your dolly and let's go," she told me. I grabbed my Chatty Cathy and held her tightly.

I heard the scraping sound of someone shoveling snow off the porch from the outside. "Open the door, Timmy!" shouted Mr. O'Brien. He was a friend of my mother's.

"Come on, jump in the truck," he instructed my brothers. He picked me up as my mother climbed into the cab of the telephone utility worker's truck. She scraped the edge of her boots on the running board as he handed me to her. "Lock the door," he told her.

"Ma, where we going?" Tim asked again. "Why are we in Mr. O'Brien's telephone truck? Dad's not gonna like this!"

"We're going on a little adventure. Okay? Just for a little while. We're even going to fly on an airplane! Whaddaya think o' that, Timmy?"

"Mommy, can we see the cockpit?" Scotty asked.

"I don't know, Scotty," answered my mother. I watched out the window as we crawled slowly through drifts of new snow.

That February, Boston's twenty-four-hour snowfall set a record—but I didn't know that. All I knew was that my mom seemed nervous and my brothers acted excited, and the grimy buildings we were passing looked like a giant had tromped alongside them and decorated them with whorls and mounds of white sparkly frosting.

"Okay, Judy. Here you go." Mr. O'Brien pulled up to South Station.

"You got cab money?"

"Yeah, we're fine," my mom answered.

He helped us out and we stood on the curb while Mommy hailed one of the two cabs sitting in the slush.

"Billerica," she instructed the cabbie. The tires skidded as we pulled away.

Ma's friend Bridgett was there at the next stop to meet us. "This should throw them off, Judy, don't you think?" she asked, as she led us outside.

There was the telephone truck again, sitting across the street. We climbed into it and Mr. O'Brien drove us to Bridgett's house. Almost no one was on the streets. I saw a car at a light ahead slide right through the intersection, its driver honking his horn.

We spent the night there. We all sat in front of the TV, but Mom and Bridgett kept making us switch the channel so they could hear the weather report. Bridgett made up pallets on the floor for the boys. I slept on the sofa. We all slept in our clothes—I had no clue where our pajamas were but I didn't care.

* * * * *

"Mo–o–m! Mrs. O'Brien says to get up!" Tim shook my mom awake and she jumped out of bed quickly.

"Come on, Lisa, time to go." She lifted me off the sofa. "I need a cup of coffee and maybe Bridgett will have some cereal for you guys."

"I've got Rice Krispies or Shredded Wheat," Bridgett announced as we trooped into the small kitchen. She poured the cereal we asked for into pink Melmac bowls.

Within ten minutes we were out the door and on our way to Boston Logan Airport. For this trip we rode in Bridgett's white Rambler. There were a few more cars on the streets than there had been the day before. They were moving slowly, but they were moving.

Bridgett pulled up to the curb and left the motor idling while she jumped out of the driver's seat, popped open the trunk, and set the box and the suitcases just inside the sliding door.

"C'mon, Tim. Scotty, watch the ice. Lisa, grab Cathy and let's go." Mom hugged her good friend as I held my Chatty Cathy doll close, not understanding the excitement but knowing something was about to happen. "I'll let you know we got to Tulsa as soon as I can find a pay phone there, okay? If you see Tommy, you know what to say: 'I don't know where they are and I don't care. Judy and I are not good friends anymore.'"

Bridgett nodded. "Okay. Now go. Talk with ya soon." She climbed into her car and we all waved as she inched the Rambler through the slush. I held Mommy's hand as we got in line in the terminal, still wondering why Mommy was acting like this adventure was such a big secret.

Judy Zerveskes Connors, 1960s and early 1970s

Tommy Connors' real last name was "Connor," but everyone called him "Tommy Connors." The only reason for the different name, as far as I know, was that "Connors" was easier to remember.[1]

Tommy was a charmer and a bad boy. He was quite the talker, on any subject. He had a reputation in Southie for two things: he was a talented featherweight boxer and he had a legendary ability to end an argument with his fists. A good Catholic girl like my mother couldn't resist the way he used to whistle at her and try to get her attention. My mother Judy was very pretty— a tall, big-busted, blonde, with long straight hair, and Lithuanian features that were just about the opposite of his. She was quiet and he was a talker. He was short and slight, with Irish good looks and curly brown hair. Tommy used to hang on the corner of D and Broadway streets and wait for her.

Judy's parents didn't know it—she didn't talk to them about what she did when she wasn't at home—but Tommy and Judy started seeing each other when Judy was fourteen or fifteen, Tommy three years older. They used to sneak around, like all Judy's friends did. Their Catholic girls' school was so strict that the students couldn't even talk to each other while they ate lunch. My mother has described how the nuns routinely slapped the girls or hit them with rulers for the smallest infraction. That atmosphere was one reason they went wild when they weren't at school. All her friends did the same things as Judy. They'd smoke and fool around with boys. Judy's mom, my Nana Frances, saw her once sitting on the stairs outside behind

---

[1]Because our real last name was Connor, there will be some discrepancies in our last name throughout this book.

Blinstrub's Restaurant with Tommy but she didn't say anything to her—I guess she didn't know what to say.

Judy did graduate high school, though, which was more than what Tommy did. She knew he was a school dropout. He was three years older than she was and already known as a ladies' man. He was also a boxer in the featherweight category, and word around Southie was that he was ferocious. She believed it. She didn't know what else he did to make money—that's something that girls in Southie didn't really ask about in those days of the late 1960s.

Judy dated some other guys during her teen years. She was even fixed up on a blind date with John Kerry, who currently serves as the United States Secretary of State. As she remembers it, he was on summer vacation from Yale at the time. She didn't think he was handsome at all, even though she could see that he was brilliant. That was before he went to Vietnam, and no one then would have guessed what he would become. They only dated a couple times—not surprising considering they had nothing in common, but he did keep contact with her over the years, calling her occasionally just to say "Hi." He even called on her in person not long after I was born. I guess that's something politicians do, keep their relationships going.

Judy was a Southie girl through and through, but she wasn't Irish. Her family's background was Lithuanian, which is the other big ethnic group in South Boston. By Southie standards, her family was pretty well off. Her parents had a summer cottage in New Hampshire and owned a two–flat building just a couple blocks from Boston Harbor and about a mile from Castle Island, which was their home. They rented out the apartment under the one in which they lived. Underneath the building were two garages, one for their car and one for the renter's—quite a luxury given that having even one garage was a rarity in Southie. Because Southie is slowly becoming gentrified now, that building is worth a fortune today. My grandparents, up until the year 2009, continued hiking up and down two flights of stairs at the ages of ninety and nine-two. My grandfather, "Papa Vinny," still made his way down those steep stairs, one inside staircase and one outside staircase every day to pick up his *Globe,* even when the outside stairs were so icy he could have easily fallen and broken a hip, or worse.

My grandfather owned Columbus Tavern a couple blocks' walk from their house. He worked long hours six days a week and carried each day's take home with him in cash. When I think of how he was never mugged or robbed, I wonder now if the locals, those on both the inside and the outside of the law, protected him because they often had a beer or two in his bar, and maybe they had an unwritten hands-off agreement in regard to him. I know he was not afraid of any of them, and he didn't share any of the gossip he heard at work, though I imagine he heard a lot about Tommy.

Judy's relationship with her parents was probably a pretty typical Southie one. She lived with them, went to Mass with them, watched TV with them, and ate meals with them. But they didn't share much conversation, and she did a lot of things behind their backs because she knew they disapproved of Tommy.

By the age of eighteen Judy had been fooling around with Tommy for quite a while. From the gossip Judy heard, she had figured out that Tommy was also playing the field. That changed when she got pregnant.

Tommy and Judy drove to New Hampshire and got married. They called soon after the ceremony and told her parents. Vinny and Frances were not happy. They considered Tommy a thug. And if that wasn't enough reason to be angry, they had already gone through the aftereffects of Judy's brother Vinny, Jr.'s teenage elopement. He had been only seventeen at the time and the marriage didn't work out. After a couple years he had ended up right back at home. When Judy called, Frances commented dryly, "This is what happens when children don't listen to their parents." Vinny said, sarcastically, "Oh, but they're in love."

Tommy and Judy came back from their short honeymoon, had a celebration with some close friends at Blinstrub's, and rented a flat on Peter Street, less than a mile from Carson Beach in one direction and the business district on Broadway in the other. It was a pretty nice place as Southie places go, a gray frame three-story building on a narrow street built up with houses and two- or three-story flats very similar to theirs. They were on the first floor and their front door faced a small porch. A friend of Judy's, her husband, and her four children lived above them—in fact, the friend's husband used to live next door to Judy's family before he married my mom's friend. Above Judy and Tommy on the third floor lived an aunt of another friend of Judy's. That interconnectedness was typical of Southie.

Judy was a typical Southie mother and wife. She and her friends, many of them from her high school, also married to local boys, stuck together. In 1974, a federal district court ordered Boston to submit to forced busing as a means of integrating its schools. When school started in September, buses carrying black students from nearby Roxbury were met by angry white crowds in South Boston. Judy was right there with her friends. When parents staged a boycott, she participated.

Otherwise, Judy's life was pretty uneventful. So she could have a girls' night out from time to time, she and a friend upstairs traded off in babysitting. Judy's friend had two healthy children and two more who had some kind of mental abnormality. Knowing now about fetal alcohol syndrome (FAS), I think that may have been the problem. They were not Down syndrome children, but had that little flat nose and face we now see in pictures of children who are born with FAS. Someone had to watch her children all the time, because they would do things like pick up matting under the carpet and eat it.

Within eight years Judy and Tommy had two boys and two girls—Renee in 1967, Timothy in March 1968, Scotty in January 1971, and me, in August 1973. Renee was a preemie and developed one of those infections that used to put preemies at so much risk. She died very soon after she was born.

As the weeks and months went by, Tommy would disappear for days and then show up at the house with a wad of money. Judy didn't know where he got it. At the time she assumed he had won the money from a boxing match he had fought in, though it could have come from anywhere. One thing is certain: Tommy was capable of doing anything it took to survive. I'll leave it at that. Southie was a tough place then.

Judy loved Tommy—but then, so did everybody, including a lot of women. She told him that there was no way she could ever go watch him in the ring—she loved him too much and it would kill her to see him getting beat up. He did well, from what she heard, and his winnings kept food on the table and a roof over their heads. But then he'd take off for days or weeks, disappear only to come home and want to step right back into being a husband and father—for a time. We kids adored him. He was a fun dad, but as for being a husband, that's a different story.

One of my favorite stories my mom tells is about one of Tommy's long durations away from home. He hadn't brought money back in a while and Judy had little food in the house. She reached a limit that led her to The Annex, a bar on Broadway that Tommy's brother Johnny owned and where Tommy and his friends hung out most of the time. With three kids in tow, she stormed into the bar, walked behind the register, slammed it open and took every dollar out exclaiming, "This is for my kids!" She looked Tommy and the others square in the eye and walked out with her wad of money. Judy was getting very tired of Tommy being gone for extended periods, and of her not knowing where he was, if he was with another woman, or even alive. She heard more and more stories about him and his "adventures" and they didn't involve her.

And then Tommy did something that violated Judy's trust in him forever, and she knew it was time to put an end to the marriage. He gave her gonorrhea. He went to a sleazy doctor friend of his and got some penicillin and put it into the Coke she was drinking. He even tried to sneak an injection into her. He told her he had caught a urinary tract infection and he was giving her the penicillin as a preventive. He sent her to the same doctor who had passed on the antibiotics to him, a guy Judy described as a "pig doctor" due to the many moral and ethical codes he broke in dealing with her. She went to another doctor and found out the truth. That was the end.

Then Judy did the one thing she had told Tommy she would never do: she went to a boxing match without him knowing beforehand she'd be there. When he saw her sitting at ringside watching him without even being upset over the beating he was taking, he knew it was over. After that, he went to the house, got his things, and moved out.

Judy didn't know where Tommy went—but she did know he was in Southie. She continued to hear stories about him. Several weeks went by and she met a man from New York who had relatives in Southie and had come to the area to work. Let's just call him "Guy"—that really was his first name.

Guy was quite a different type from Tommy. He was tall and dark and, though he wasn't a biker, he wore a leather jacket, had longish hair, and looked like one. Actually, he looked like he wouldn't put up with any nonsense from anyone. Well. . .Guy was at the Peter Street flat one fall evening and decided to walk to the Supreme Market. It was a two minutes' walk and he should have been there and back in just a few minutes. After two hours, Judy was frantic. She knew something bad had happened to him.

Then Peter, one of Tommy's three brothers, called her and said, "I don't know a thing about what happened, Judy, except what I've heard. Guy's been in a fight. I'm not involved."

Peter's claim did the opposite of setting her mind at ease. It made her think that, yes, he was involved in some way. But how could she call the police? She knew Tommy was behind whatever had happened, no question. She walked the floor, not knowing what to do.

At about five o'clock the following morning Guy stumbled in, looking as if he had had quite a night. He told her that Tommy had jumped him on the street outside the grocery store. Guy had knocked Tommy down and then Tommy's brother Jimmy had entered the fight. He put a gun to Guy's head and the two of them threw him into a car and drove him to the bus station. They saw to it that he got on the bus back to New York and told him not to come back to Southie.

As my mom says, this sounds like a stupid story but it's true. Guy got off the bus somewhere on the way to New York and bought a ticket back to Boston.

"Judy, we can't stay here," he told her. "I'm heading out. You have your choice of where we go—Oregon or Oklahoma. I'll go out and get a job and you can follow me in a month or two."

It didn't take long for Judy to decide. She had to get as far away from Tommy as she could. People were already hinting and she was becoming convinced there was a contract out on both Guy and her. She knew the local stories and she knew if there was a hit ordered on her, she wouldn't have been the first girlfriend, mistress, or wife who ended up dead when she did something to anger or alienate her boyfriend or husband, nor would she be the last.[2]

It was the next day that one of Judy's close friends, Bridgett, received the bouquet of black roses with the note attached to it that said, "Just a warning. Keep Judy away from that biker." It sounds like a scene from *The Godfather*, but Judy took the note seriously because she knew what Tommy was capable of.

So Guy and Judy made plans. Now that I think of it, I wonder why the choice between just those two "O" states. Why not Ohio? I can't answer that. My mom told me later she chose Oklahoma because at least it would be a little easier to get back to Boston if she needed to—not that she planned to––she was too scared of what Tommy might do. She was convinced he had put out a contract not just on Guy, but on her, as well.

And then the record snowfall that February of 1978 imprisoned us in our flat. It would have been kind of fun had my mom not been so frightened of what our father might do. All of us in the three-story building shared what food we had and together we watched the TV, which, surprisingly, still worked. We couldn't see out the window, and the snow piled on the stoop was so heavy and high we could not budge the door.

After a couple days of being snowbound, Bridgett's husband, Joe, was able to get us out late in the evening. His work truck, a telephone repair truck, was a great cover and allowed us to escape without being noticed.

We took a couple of suitcases and left the only home the four of us had ever known. From Southie to another kind of South—Tulsa—and a new life. Only the passage of time would reveal whether the new life would be a happy one. And for many years my only memory of my father would be the three words he said to me the last time I saw him: "You're so beautiful."

---

[2]For a recent online article about the grisly slaying just a few years later in 1981 of one of the girfriends, see http://www.bostonherals.com/news/regional/view.bg?articleid=1184168.

My father, me on his chest, and my two brothers. This is my father's treasure and he cherished it all those years we were separated. It is the only picture he had of all four of us.

NO JUDY, NO KIDS, 1978

By his own admission Tommy was a volatile man. His ex-wife Judy had just disappeared and had taken their three kids. He wasn't too worried about the boys—after all, they were boys. He had already prepared them: "There may come a day when we can't see each other anymore. Your ma might want you to have a new daddy. Just remember, I'm your daddy."

The boys could take care of themselves. Tommy had always been a little guy and as the youngest of four brothers, it's what he had always had to do after his own father left his mother when he was a baby. He was too small to play the traditional "boy" sports, so he took up boxing. He learned to fight and he was good at it, both in the streets and in the ring.

But his beautiful little girl. What would it be like for her to grow up without a father? Girls need someone to watch over them, to stick up for them, to protect them. That's what any father would do for his little girl, he thought. So he was out to get the person who had taken her away from him.

His older brother Jimmy and he had let that biker Judy was hanging out with know that he better not show up in Southie again. No one would have wanted to cross Jimmy. Tommy was tough, but Jimmy was several giant steps ahead of him. He had been convicted of the murder of a local thug and had been sentenced to a "natural" ["for the rest of your natural life"] to be served at the state maximum-security prison in Walpole. Jimmy had been released about five years before on a John Doe writ that was responsible for the reduction in sentences for several thousand prison inmates. The document gave them the opportunity to change their pleas and Jimmy took advantage of it. Although by that time, his mind had been messed up permanently by booze and drugs, he was still Tommy's brother and brothers stick by brothers in Southie.

In those days in lower Southie, James "Whitey" Bulger's gang more or less called the shots when it came to enforcing a *de facto* behavior code. People were so interconnected that South Boston was like a little fiefdom of its own. People watched out for each other. All Tommy had to do was to ask Judy's Peter Street neighbors to report on her comings and goings and he found out all he needed to know. Tommy got the word from one informant that Guy had left the flat one evening to buy cigarettes. Tommy knew what Guy was wearing and spotted him right away.

Jimmy waited in Tommy's parked station wagon as Tommy jumped out. "Did you get cigarettes for Judy?" he asked Guy calmly.

Guy answered right away. "Yeah, I got 'em right here." He stood on the sidewalk in his leather jacket and boots, and a small flame flared up as he lit a cigarette for himself. He didn't look like he was shaking.

Tommy hit him right square in the mouth. "I hit him with a fury," Tommy said later. "He went up in the air, came down. He was making sounds like, 'aaaah.' He was holding his face. I dragged him to my station wagon. That's kidnapping. Now my brother starts in on him and says, 'Well, why don't we just end this right now.'

"I said, 'Please, Jimmy, people, they know us. Plus, I don't wanna blame it all on him. It's mostly my fault.' But I couldn't give up the idea that there was a new father there with with my wife. See, I couldn't give up. I could give up losing her. I could deal with that. It would'a been tough, but you know? I could deal with that. But a new male figure that's taking my place. .. that's what triggered the gasoline in a way of speaking. I threatened him, whatever. I told him his brains were straw if I ever saw him again."

Tommy pulled out of the parking space, his brother holding Guy captive with a knife at his throat. "To make a long story short, I told Guy Jimmy had a gun. Jimmy didn't really have one but the creep was beyond knowing what the truth was and what wasn't. He was crying; he was shaking like a leaf. I reached over and took his wallet and his keys. I took out a $100 bill and his Social Security card and driver's license and threw everything else out the window. 'I know who you are and I'll know where you are if you come back here,' I warned him. We drove him to the bus station and walked him in. I paid for a ticket to his family's home in New York with the money and we made sure he got on the bus."

But he must have come back in spite of the threats. He had fixed up something with Judy, Tommy was sure of it.

Tommy couldn't eat and he couldn't sleep. He loved that girl. She was a nice girl—like his mother—not street smart, but nice. He knew he had ruined his chances with Judy. He didn't know the technical term for what he was and what caused him to be so unfaithful to her, but he knew he had a big appetite for sex and he went about satisfying it. It had nothing to do with not getting enough at home. It was just the way he was.

And this time it had come back to kick him in the teeth. If he had known he'd lose his wife because of going to a stag party, maybe he wouldn't have gone. But he had, and he had received the gift that can keep on giving.

"I got the clap," Tommy admitted. "A doctor friend got me cleaned out, but if I had given it to Judy I know I'd just get it again." Tommy had tried to be casual about it, telling her that he had a urinary tract infection and wanted to keep her from getting it, but apparently she wasn't as naïve as he had thought.

Judy was a lost cause. He had a lot of love to give. There was nothing else to do but look for love somehow, somewhere, and take out his frustration and loneliness as he was used to doing, in the ring. "You can't love for two, you know?" Tommy explained when someone asked him why he wasn't with his wife anymore. After a few weeks he began to step out with the women again. He continued to ask around about Judy and the kids, but found out nothing of substance.

Then a slight acquaintance in the neighborhood approached him. "I know where your ex-wife is. If you want to know, it'll cost you this much," and he named a figure. Tommy flat out refused. He spotted Judy's mother

Frances a couple times as she was walking home from the Supreme Market and stopped his car to talk with her, but didn't pump her for information.

"If you ever need anything, Mrs. Zerveskes, you just let me know and I'll take care of it for you, okay?"

She nodded and said "Thanks," and walked on quickly as if to pass on the message, *I can tell you nothing more.*

The months and then the years passed. Life in South Boston went on much as it always had. It was a world unto itself, with its own self-appointed ruling party and its own enforcers of the law that were only coincidentally, it often seemed, connected with the officially elected ones. Tommy graduated from prize-fighting to coaching, telling himself that if he couldn't be with his boys, at least he could mentor some other boys who needed a father figure.

Meanwhile, the salt air and bitter cold of the winds whipping around Fort Independence on Castle Island became less than memories to me, for I was too young to feel any ties to the city in which I was born. My entire stock of memories centered around three meager words that I thought I remembered my father saying to me, though I wasn't sure where or when I had heard them: "You're so beautiful."

From Southie to the South, 1978

"This is a fresh start for us, Tim," Mom answered my brother. I could count up to twenty and I knew he asked her twenty, maybe even twenty-eleven, times why we had to leave Boston. Mom's friend Guy was a part of our lives from that very first rainy February day, though it would be more than two years before he and Mom actually got married at the Tulsa City Hall. He led us to the Tulsa city bus, which we rode to an intersection near downtown Tulsa. "There's the motel," he pointed. "Come on."

I carried Cathy, while Guy and my brothers dragged the bags and the box.

The rooms opened to the outside. In front of the parking area a rusty swing set sat on a patch of brown grass, the wet swings moving slowly back and forth, back and forth, in the chilly winter breeze. Cigarette butts littered the ground around two turquoise metal chairs by the door.

"Mom, how long are we going to be here?" Tim asked. Mom didn't answer.

"Here's where you'll sleep," Guy said. "You boys will share that bed. I asked the manager to bring in a rollaway for Lisa." The boys staked out their claims—I was too tired to care. "I'll see you in the morning," Guy said. "Lock that door and make sure you dead-bolt it—just in case." He stood in the door, lighted a cigarette, and looked slowly both ways before saying, "'Night, Judy."

"Ma'am, I have the cot." A woman's voice on the other side of the door prompted my mother to unlatch the dead-bolt. Her voice sounded strange––sort of slow, with the "I" sounding more like "Ah" and "have" sounding like "hay–ave." It was like nothing I had ever heard. My mother cautiously opened the door a crack and then let the woman inside. The bed made up for me, I climbed under the sheet, putting my Cathy on the thin pillow beside me. Mom pulled the beige blanket up to my chin but I still had a hard time settling down.

"Mommy, where's Daddy?" I asked.

"He's in Boston, Lisa. Now try to go to sleep," she answered. "Scotty and Timmy, quit talking," she said. "We have to enroll you in school tomorrow," she said, turning off the light between the two beds.

As I drifted off to sleep, I heard Mom unlatch the dead-bolt, latch it again, unlatch it again, and then latch it again, as if to make sure it really worked. The third time she opened the door and stood in the doorway as if watching for someone.

"Hey, Timmy! Quit hogging the covers!" whispered Scotty. "Mom, it's cold in here!"

Mom locked and dead-bolted the door once more. Thus began our first night in the South.

Who was my mom looking for? I didn't know then. As the years passed, though, I fit the puzzle pieces together and realized that the missing piece was my father. And he was a piece my mother hoped she'd never find. When we finally got a car, she'd look behind her every time she turned off the ignition. When we got home after being gone somewhere, she'd scout out each empty room.

"Mom, he's not going to find us," Tim would tell her. "Cool it. He's not coming all the way out here."

"You don't know your father like I know your father," she'd answer. "Just make sure the door's locked."

Wherever we were, I had the feeling that he might be watching us, because it was obvious Mom thought so. Was he? If he were, he kept himself hidden very well.

THE ACCIDENT, 1980

"Omigod," I heard my mother say.

The policeman stood at the front door holding a wallet in his hands. "Ma'am, is this your husband's?" He asked her. Then he said, "He was hit while he was walking across the street at the light. He was taken by ambulance to Hillcrest Hospital. I can take you there if you don't have a car."

Mom grabbed her big blue denim purse. "Tim, you're going to have to stay here and not take off with your friends. Keep an eye on Scotty and Lisa. I have to get to the hospital. I'll call you from there. Make sure you are near enough to hear the phone."

They weren't married at that time, not yet, but everyone assumed they were. We had moved into a shabby one-bedroom duplex on South Quincy, about a mile from downtown Tulsa. Guy had been a chef before we moved to Tulsa, but I don't recall where he worked when we joined him there, or if he did. He was a quiet man who didn't talk to us kids much. In his free time, if he wasn't sprawled on the couch reading, he was at the library, and if he wasn't at the library, he was listening to a record album on the little turntable that sat next to the small portable television in the living room.

He had taken a walk down to the Utotem just a couple blocks from the duplex where a car came through the intersection at a high speed and hit him.[3] His injuries were extensive, and when Mom came back that evening she told us Guy was in a coma. She explained that he was unconscious and the doctors didn't know when he'd wake back up.

---

[3]As far as I know, the person who committed the hit-and-run was never found or prosecuted.

Mom told us, "I may not be here when you get home from school tomorrow, but you are not to go anywhere. Do you hear me?"

Five days went by during which we saw her very little. "Guy opened his eyes and seemed to recognize me," she told us. He was in the hospital for another six weeks. Then one day when we got home from school there he was, lying on the couch watching TV.

My mother married Guy when I was seven years old. He was not a mean man, but the car accident left him with some residual brain damage. He had frequent Grand Mal seizures that kept him from being able to hold a stable job or get a driver's license. I recall what a seizure experience was like, seeing him have them on several occasions. There was one incident when I even put a spoon in his mouth to bring his tongue forward to help him not to choke. Those seizures are scary to witness for a child, but Mom told me that they weren't as serious as they looked and they wouldn't kill him, so I guess I got used to them.

I don't think Guy ever did, though. While his physical condition seemed to improve a little over the years, he seemed to become more disinterested in us, even secretive. I don't know where he got his money—I do know he was able to get disability from the government, so that's probably where the money came from—but he managed to buy booze. Eventually, his unhappiness over not being able to provide for his wife and her children led him to become an alcoholic. He would sneak behind a dumpster and turn a bottle upside down into his throat. I used to go out and look under the dumpster, to see how many bottles were there. There would be several, some of them shattered. The green and brown shards of glass glittered at me like slinty cat eyes in the late afternoon sun and I knew they represented money we needed, now gone forever.

* * * * *

"Tim, Scotty, Lisa, come here. I need to get to work. Now you're going to have to do what Guy tells you to do," Mom explained. "I have to work nights because the night shift pays fifty cents extra an hour. I can't turn that down. We need the money."

Mom had found a nurse's aide course offered through a local hospital. When she passed her state certification test, the hospital quickly hired her. Guy didn't treat us badly—he just more or less ignored us. He didn't seem to care much about what we were up to as long as we stayed out of trouble and didn't involve him in what we were doing. We played outside and roamed the neighborhood during the daytime hours when Mom was home because she slept during the day and we had to be quiet.

Their bed was in the dining room and to get to the bathroom we had to tiptoe through it. We knew she had to get her sleep and, in fact, she and Guy insisted that we play outside during the day so that she could rest. The rule was that we were to stay outside until dark. As time passed, it became easier and more pleasant to stay outside or spend even bigger blocks of time with friends. Some friends' families actually even ate dinner together sometimes, something we very rarely did, and I ate with them more and more often.

I dressed in Scott's and Tim's hand-me-down t-shirts and Wranglers. I don't recall having new clothes often or anything that looked feminine. I looked the part of a tomboy, which I guess I was. I got in the habit of following my two brothers around. I would run after them and try to enter into their games of hide-and-seek with their friends and they would try to ditch me. "Go home, Lisa. We don't want girls," they'd tell me.

I remember the first time, though it would not be the last, that they simply abandoned me in an empty lot near downtown Tulsa and left me to find my way home alone. I was seven or eight. I crawled out from behind a bush where I had been hiding for the game of hid-and-seek to find myself alone. It was early evening and it would be dark soon. I started backtracking the same way I had followed Scotty and Tim earlier that day. I knew I had to hurry.

A street person approached me and I pretended I didn't notice him. "Missy, do you have a quarter?" "Hey, little girl, where do you live?" asked another man slouching against a lamppost a few blocks down the street. I began running and kept on until I saw the lighted lamps in our living room window up ahead of me. By the time I got to the duplex, it was dark outside and Mom had already left for work. Nobody had tried to find me.

Being left to watch out for myself those times probably toughened me, but it isolated me, as well. Besides, Mom and I didn't talk to each other much, and I talked with Guy even less. When I made friends with some neighborhood girls and spent time in their homes, I realized that our family was not like theirs. I began to feel more at ease with them than I did at home. I think Tim and Scotty felt the same way, because with every passing year they seemed to be home less than the year before.

I was in charge of keeping the wash caught up when Mom didn't have time or was too tired to do it. We had one of those washing machines that needed to be wheeled over to the sink. We didn't have a dryer for many years, so I hung the clothes on the line outside during warm days and during the winters we strung a line in the living room.

Even though I wasn't supposed to be in the house while my mother slept, I spent a lot of time very quietly observing her as she slept. She often had her mouth wide open in her heavy sleep. I knew she was tired and I always understood without being told that working the night shift was a tough thing to do. Once in a while she talked about the kinds of things she did. Nurse's aides had to clean up foul-smelling messes, and they changed bed pans and helped the patients to the bathroom. They had to pick up heavy things, too. Sometimes they worked with people who were nearing death and often those who did eventually pass away, and sometimes they just held the hands of those people as they died. There were times that my mother was the first person to tell a loved one about the person's passing, and I wondered what that would be like.

There was a funny smell in the hospital, but occasionally we'd stop there to pick up Mom's paycheck and she'd drop me at the children's play area while she went to get it. I liked it there because there were always some fun toys, and toys were not something my mom or my stepfather spent money on. Sometimes I would see children there who were dragging portable IVs along behind them. Some were bandaged up, while others were missing hair because of this thing I learned about in school called cancer that people often died from. I remember seeing a mother's tears run down her cheeks as she played with her child. I wondered what it would be like to have someone cry about me.

A Boy's Life in Southie, 1950s and 1960s

I am my father's daughter. That statement is obvious and true—he passed on his DNA to me. That fact begs the question: In what ways am I like my father? I certainly didn't look like him. Another question occurs to me: How could a man who I didn't even know have influenced my life?

My mother has made a statement to me many times. It might sound like a put-down but it's not: "Where did you come from? You're not part of this family." She says it with a smile and she does not mean it in a derogatory sense. What she means is, your personality is so different from mine and from the Zerveskes side of the family. It's sure not from me!

The best way to answer my questions about myself is to begin by filling in some details about Tommy Connors so his personality emerges. Everyone is the result of where they grew up to some extent. The daughter of a New Englander, I grew up in the mid-South. I knew little of the Irish Catholic culture of South Boston. That influence was not in my life, but there were some Southern-flavored influences that shaped my values and personality. I also know Tommy's own early experiences in a Roxbury cold-water flat and a housing project in South Boston influenced the kind of man he became and is today. Mix each person's environment with heredity and you have a uniquely seasoned stew. Yet most stews have some similar ingredients, right? The questions that I have wanted to answer for years are, "what kind of person is my dad?" and "how am I like him?"

As a child, I knew I had a father, and I assumed he was alive. I knew almost nothing else about him other than that my grandparents called him a gangster and my mother was terrified he'd find out where we were. She never got over that fear. It wasn't until years later that I learned more about him.

Tommy's life began on November 14, 1945 in Roxbury, Massachusetts, less than five miles from the house on Peter Street where he and Judy lived after they got married. He was the youngest of four boys, small in stature like both his mother and his father, who were first generation Irish Americans. First came Johnny, then Jimmy, then Peter, and then Tommy.

Tommy's father was a hustler and a money maker. He was, at various times, a fireman or a taxicab driver, doing whatever he could do to make money. He was street smart and not surprisingly for that time, Tommy's mother Agnita, whose maiden name was Doherty, wasn't. She was a nice, religious girl who was an only child to her Irish American parents.

The match was not made in heaven. How they got together in the first place is something I don't know, but the marriage must have been pretty contentious because they divorced—almost unheard of for a South Boston Irish Catholic family in those days of the late 1940s. Tommy was only a baby when his father moved out. He only saw him occasionally after that.

The Roxbury flat they lived in was so cold that the toilet water would freeze and they'd have to pee out the window. As a divorcee, Tommy's mother had to get special permission to enable the four boys to attend parochial school there.

From the very first, Tommy had trouble learning to read. He related an incident that happened when he was ten or eleven sheds light on why he hated school so much:

"I'd read backwards, from right to left instead of left to right. Now I know that's dyslexia, but no one seemed to know what was wrong with me then. I tried to get a jump on the assignments by doing the ones I knew were coming up before school. One morning one of the nuns, the one who had held me back in the third grade two times, caught me doing some work outside the school door and marched me into the coatroom.

"Take down your pants," she demanded.

"Okay."

"Now take down your underwear."

"I ain't. My ma told me never to take down my underwear for anybody." The rumors were out that priests had been known to put their fingers up little boys' rectums (a rumor I also heard years later, from some of the boys I mentored in boxing), and Ma had heard those stories many years ago, too, I guess.

"No, Sister, I ain't."

She called in the priest, Father MacIntyre (not his real name). He made me repeat what I had said to Sister MaryAnne. I added, "Father, I'm sorry. I was just trying to get ahead in my schoolwork." I repeated my mother's warning to me and my brothers.

"Tom, I'm going to tell you once, take down your pants now, or I'm going to drop the wrath of God on you."

"No, Father. I'm sorry, but I can't."

Bam! And out of the blue . . . he punched me in the face and knocked me right on my ass! I passed out for a few seconds. Then I picked myself up and ran out the entrance and home to Ma. My eye was swollen. I had the start of a shiner.

"Tom, what am I going to do with you? Come on, let's go back to the school and I'll talk with Father MacIntyre," she said, grabbing me by the hand.

By the end of the day not only was I out, but my three brothers were, too. When she tried to smooth over the situation, Father MacIntyre swore at her and told her to take us all and get out. So she did. One incident with one kid, and we were all out.

Agnita decided to apply for public housing and she got accepted into Columbia Point at the tip of South Boston. Located on Boston Harbor, the project was considered a step up from Roxbury, though because it was an uncomfortable mixture of races a fight was always simmering between one person or group and another one. Columbia Point had more than 1500 units. It was the largest government housing project in Boston and one of the largest in the entire United States. At that time it housed working class families. Later, the mix slowly shifted to many who were poor and unemployed, and the property began to go downhill due to neglect by the Boston Housing Authority and other factors. When Agnita and her boys moved in, though, it was hard to judge who loved the hot baths more, Agnita or her four sons.

Life in Columbia Point was an improvement, but then two months in a row someone stole Agnita's welfare check. During the long weeks before the next check, she and the boys ate cheap pound potatoes and little else. Agnita was asthmatic—a condition Tommy and his brothers all suffered from at one point or another. Her lack of education and poor health meant she was only able to take menial housekeeping and cleaning crew jobs when she was able to work.

Observing his mother's hard life, Tommy decided two things: He was going to make her laugh whenever he could. Always an entertaining and amusing storyteller, Tommy challenged himself to make a smile cross his mother's tired face. He also decided that he was going to figure out a way to make some money.

But how would he pull that off? Education didn't look like it would hold the answer. He was about done with school. He had had enough of being forced to read out loud and stumbling over both the words and their meaning. He couldn't understand why it was so hard for him and no one seemed to care. Yeah, they put him in special school, special classes—but the teachers seemed both baffled and impatient.

"I was so frustrated that when the teacher would tell me to stand up and read, I would be so mad that I would want to beat up everybody. And anyone that ever mentioned to me I couldn't read, I would beat up," he said later.

Not being able to communicate through the written word, he began to carry around "a huge chip" on his shoulder, his body language and attitude daring someone to knock it off. He decided that God must have something against him.

Thirteen-year-old Tommy was a compact package of testosterone, anger, and nervous energy. What to do with all that? He couldn't excel in football, too small—or basketball, too short. The only sport he could excel in was boxing—because they went per pound.

In seventh grade Tommy simply quit going to school. He began running up to ten miles a day to get himself in condition. So began the next chapter of Tommy's life, the years of Tommy the Boxer.

THE YEARS OF TOMMY THE BOXER, LATE 1960S–1980S

Walk up and down South Boston streets today and you'll see old brick buildings with signs posted that list boxing lessons for boys and Irish step dancing lessons for girls. Those lessons have been a part of local culture for many years. By the time Tommy was a young teenager he was sparring and training at McDonough's gym and other places. He got very good at the sport—he participated in Golden Gloves competitions and usually won in the featherweight class. In his late teens Tommy qualified for the Olympics, but he broke his hand in a street fight. He was always ready to take a swing, and did, when someone got smart with him. That particular fight sidelined him for a few weeks.

Like many other young men of South Boston, Tommy also found some security by fitting in with local culture—which meant being peripherally connected to the *de facto* Irish don of Southie, Whitey Bulger and his gang. Not that he ever officially or purposely joined up with them—it was just that relationships were so interwoven in South Boston that if a man lived his life inside its confines it was almost inevitable that he would eventually become somehow entangled in the web of shakedowns, threats, and even murders that were just part of life there. As Tommy puts it, "Everything in this town was very, very tight. No one could say anything about anything. If you said anything about Whitey, it would get right back. It would get right back to him."

Bulger and his associates had their fingers in both crime and legitimate businesses. If you were an owner of a local market, for example, you might be "encouraged" to pay a monthly protection fee to one of Whitey's "assistants," and you needed to be careful not to complain about that "service."[4] Or maybe you would be recruited to be one of the assistants yourself. In some way, at some time, you'd run across the people who really ran South Boston. So it was a good idea to make sure you kept your mouth shut and learned how to protect yourself.

Tommy did both. Tommy was a talker, but he learned who to talk to and who not to talk to. He also became good at using his hands. He had a survivor's instinct, but what really ignited the fuel in the tank for Tommy

Tommy Connors preparing for a fight.

---

[4]See Howie Carr, *The Brothers Bulger* (New York; Warner Books, 2006) chapter 13 for an account of how his gang extorted one business owner.

was rage. His anger at himself, at God, at his lack of opportunities, often flared up into a flame that traveled down the circuit from his resentment to his fists.

When he wasn't training Tommy worked at The Annex. As he pumped beer on tap he listened to the local boxers and promoters and made some connections. Before he and Judy got married, while he was still a teenager, he went pro and sometimes the purse was pretty good.

He was participating in scheduled bouts when he met Judy, though he didn't talk much about them to her and she didn't go to see him box. He worked hard and was successful at strengthening his left hand so that he could be a two-handed boxer, one that could come at the opponent from both sides.

In 1970, twenty-five-year-old Tommy Connors, the married man, won a bout at the Boston Garden, the mecca of the boxing world. Bostonians considered the Garden the Queen of Boxing, with New York's Madison Square Garden being the King. It was the quickest professional bout in the history of the Garden up to that date. He knocked out the opponent in thirteen seconds including the count.

He was at the peak of his career. He would look in the mirror and his fierce expression scared even him. Though he had a huge appetite for sex, he refused to do anything to satisfy it when a bout was to occur. He fought a ten-round bout at the Garden prior to a closed circuit broadcast of a Cassius Clay bout, right around the time Clay became Muhammad Ali, and he won it.

Over the years of his boxing career, Tommy racked up the following statistics:

- 20 pro fights

- 17 knockouts

- 18 wins

- 1 loss

- 1 draw

Though he boxed professionally for years, he was never knocked out, never hurt. Still, Tommy Connors, by then with a family to support, looked into his future and saw hard reality: There was no security in his future as a boxer. His children needed to eat and it seemed everyone was trying to con him. It was like a racket, he thought. He was frustrated and that made him more eager to punch people, to fight people.

He got into some nasty disagreements outside the gym, some at The Annex, though he told himself he never picked on anyone that didn't have it coming and he never went after anyone who couldn't fight. He stayed away from booze and drugs, having seen in his brother's life the damage that both can do. He was getting a reputation around the neighborhood. He got himself a pit bull puppy and he would take the dog with him when he worked the day shift. One day a cab driver came in for a drink. Tommy described what happened:

The guy must have weighed 350 pounds. He was half out of his mind because someone stole one of his cabs and abandoned it at Cape Cod. He had to go all the way there to get it and he was in the mood to take it out on someone, anyone who was an easy target. So he hit me and then started picking on my little pit bull. He shouldn't have done that. It was a bad time for this to happen but I let him have it. Scared the guy half to death. It was a bad time—I was a married man and my wife wasn't happy—but he hit me first. But it was still a bad time for this to happen. And then he said I tried to rob him!

Tommy had to get a lawyer. The cab driver said that Tommy was drunk and tried to shake him down, but the lawyer countered with the argument that it was a well-known fact that Tommy wasn't a drinker, and even if he had been the so-called fight occurred at twelve noon, during his working hours.

When he and the lawyer appeared at the arraignment, the lawyer said sarcastically to the judge, ""Just look at Tommy and then at the accuser. How could Tommy, all of maybe 140 pounds, be a threat to this guy?"

The judge threw the case out. So Tommy got lucky on that one. Yet the rage was still there. Able to keep it in check enough not to actually beat up on Judy or his three children, he broke furniture and lamps, instead. Or he'd take off for days at a time, during which he'd channel the anger into sexual energy, finding release by burning it off in the arms of women he'd meet in bars or through friends.

It was probably inevitable that he'd run into James "Whitey" Bulger at one time or another, because Bulger, like most South Boston men, liked to go to the fights. He describes his first meeting with the crime boss. It took place in a restaurant:

My trainer, Jimmy Connally, brought me in to have a steak dinner before a fight one night. The first time I meet this guy I know him [who he was—I had heard about him]. He comes over to me and says, "Who you lookin' at?"

"You're the one lookin' at me!" I said. "I'm in here to have a meal. I have to fight tonight."

He said, "I don't care about your fight. I'm going home."

I said, "Come to the fight. Get close to ringside. I'll put him in your lap." I almost said, "I'll put you in his lap!" But I didn't.

It became a little confrontational.

He said, "I don't like you, pal. Do you know who I am?"

A couple of the guys in the bar stepped in between us—I think they wanted to stop a fight they saw coming.

I said, "I know who you are. I ain't scared o' ya." He looked at me real hard and he stepped back. He thought he could intimidate me.

I said to him, "I'm just sitting here and having dinner. I'll leave."

He said, "I hope you get knocked out tonight."

I said, "You know something? Sit at ringside. I'll lay him right in your lap. You play with me, you get burned."

"You play with me, you die," he says.

From that night I just stayed away from the guy. But he must have heard of my fighting ability. I just stayed away from the man, though. I did speak to him if I saw him on the street. He had halitosis.

And he'd say something to me, and actually he smelled like he ate shit. I mean ate it out of the toilet. And I almost said to him once, "Hey, you smell like you ate shit, kid."

And I stopped . . . and I shut right up. 'Cause, you know, I didn't want to beat the guy up. Well, I thought I could beat anybody up. But I didn't want to beat up on him. Because that guy, you'd have to kill him.

Tommy didn't see Bulger at the venue where he boxed that night when he dared him to come and sit in the front row. He did see him on the streets or in local hangouts from time to time but he never purposely tried to get into his inner circle.

Even a connection-once-removed with Bulger and his cronies would be enough to get him into serious trouble later, but he didn't realize that during the years of Tommy the Boxer.

A New Kind of Danger, 1970s and Early 1980s

What a world away from Southie is Tulsa. The people in both places speak "American"—but the people who were born and raised in South Boston and Tulsa have such distinctive accents and such different everyday phrases and slang terms that when visitors from other countries try to communicate with people in either place thinking they'll be speaking "English" with them—the textbook language they studied in textbooks in Japan or Germany Russia or Argentina—what they find is that they cannot understand what the people in Southie or Tulsa are saying.

People in Southie and Tulsa are different in many ways, some of them reflected in the terms they use: A priest is called "Father" in my dad's town, while in Tulsa you might hear a pastor referred to as "Brother Smith." People in Southie go to Mass; people in Tulsa go to church. Southie restaurants serve "tonics;" Tulsa restaurants serve the same thing, only they call it "pop" or "soda." In Southie houses have cellars; in Tulsa they have basements.

I could go on and on, and I've not even gotten started on the accents themselves. I think they also reflect differences in the people. The Southie man, woman, or child speaks rapidly, with the "a's" flattened and the "r's" missing in a word like "yard," the dialect reflecting the harsh weather and the poverty. In Oklahoma, a gentle drawing out of some words like "have" into what sounds like two syllables ("hay-ave") suggests to me the humidity, heat, and slower pace of the rural background of many of the natives.

Here's the thing, though: There are good people and bad people in both places. Both Southie and Tulsa, as with everywhere else in the world, is home to kind people, good people, and people who prey on others, bad people.

My mother thought she was protecting us by leaving South Boston and an ex-husband who was supposedly out for her blood. Yet not long after we moved into the duplex we would call home for several years, I walked into a kind of danger that I doubt I would have been exposed to in Southie. The reason—my brothers and I were by ourselves much of the time, unsupervised. Things happened that nobody would have even thought of doing to Tommy Connors' kids back in Southie.

I am not at liberty to reveal information about my brothers' experiences in Oklahoma, but when I was about six, a really nice man we called "Mr. Jimmy" lived on the other side of our duplex. He was very kind to us. My brothers were in and out of his side of the duplex all the time. He would make Kool-Aid, give us each a big metal glass of it, and put out bowls of pretzels and chips, and we'd sit and watch The Mike Douglas Show after school with him.

One day I went in by myself and Mr. Jimmy told me I could lie down on the couch since no one else was there. He turned on the TV and left me for a couple of minutes and when he came back he told me he had a surprise for me.

"Close your eyes, okay?" He said. "No peeking."

It's hard to describe what I felt next. It was an unknown sensation. It was cold and hard, like a metal rod inside my shorts. "Lie still, Lisa," he said.

His fingers fumbled around between my legs and I felt something cold at the top of my thigh. Then it seemed to be inside me and I felt like I had to go pee. I opened my eyes into the smallest of slits and saw that he had his eyes closed and was moving something around inside my shorts with one hand while his other hand was rubbing, rubbing himself below his waist. And the metal thing hurt. It hurt bad. I was afraid to move. I wanted to cry but I didn't know if I would get in trouble for crying or not.

"Okay, Lisa, I'm done. You probably shouldn't tell anyone about this," he said. He helped me up and ruffled my hair in a brotherly way. "Want some grape Kool-Aid?"

"No, I gotta go," I said.

I hurt down below in a way I had never felt before. I ran past Guy, who was dozing on the couch, and into the bathroom.

Blood! I could see that the water in the toilet bowl was red. I started to cry. I must have gotten pretty loud.

"Do you not hear Lisa crying? What is wrong with you?" I heard Mom yelling at Guy, and next thing I knew she was standing over me as I sat on the toilet. "What happened?"

"Mr. Jimmy stuck something inside me," I wailed.

By this time Guy was standing next to my mom. "I'll go kill that son of a bitch!" he yelled.

My mom helped me get myself cleaned up. "Now Lisa, you stay here," she warned me. "I'm going to go see what Guy is up to over there."

But she didn't have to. Guy stomped in, rubbing his fist. "He won't be doing that again anytime soon," he said. "I'm calling the cops." A few minutes later I pulled the curtains back enough to see as two uniformed men took Mr. Jimmy in handcuffs and shoved him into the back seat of a police car.

I was afraid to even go outside after that, but it wasn't long before I didn't have to worry about him because he moved. Nothing was ever said about what he had done to me. As far as I know neither Mom nor Guy pressed charges. Of course, we didn't talk about much of anything, let alone anything so personal, in our house.

As my memory returns to that shabby duplex, I realize that Tim, Scotty, and I were both streetwise and ignorant. We knew bad things happened sometimes. We knew kids they had happened to. But the truth is that no one actually sat down with us—at least not with me—and explained anything about pedophiles or child molesters. There were no lectures about how your body is your own private property or about how no one has the right to touch you where you don't want to be touched. And after enduring something no little girl should have to endure, I got no counseling afterwards. Consequently, I kept this memory hidden, untouched, and unexamined for years. It's only now that I have chosen to share this part of my story.

A little knowledge would *not* have been a dangerous thing—it would have kept us from some pain. My brothers went through some painful things, too, but since this story is mine, I am not elaborating on the events that affected their lives. Nor do I know many of the details of their early life experiences because I was enough younger than they were that they ran in different circles, and I only heard or saw bits and pieces of their lives.

I think of my dad as a boy in Southie—little Tommy Connors, ordered by a priest to pull his pants down in a parochial school coat room. Predators are everywhere, and it is a parent's duty to protect his or her children. Too many bury their heads in the sand and assume that a "nice" neighbor, or teacher, or preacher, or Boy Scout leader would never be a pedophile. Once a child has been damaged by a predator, it is too late to suddenly become aware. Years later, my dad told me that after my mom left he had not been worried about his sons being able to take care of themselves—Tommy's world was, and probably still is, a man's world, where the tough survive. But he would think from time to time of his daughter and worry about her, knowing that men can be ruthless in taking what they want. He remembered his beautiful little girl and assumed that her childish beauty would only increase as she grew up—after all, his ex-wife was a knockout. How was his little Lisa making it through the years? He wished he knew, but finding out was a lost cause.

If he had known what Mr. Jimmy had done to me, I wonder what my father would have thought; I think I know what he would have *done.*

WANTING AND NOT GETTING, 1980S

The quarters looked like little silver tops as they sparkled in the sunlight that streamed through the store window. Tim and Scotty each had taken one out of their jeans pocket and tapped them with their thumb and forefinger, making them spin around. The quarters' momentum spun out and each one slowed and then stopped, and lay flat on the Formica-topped Rexall Drugstore counter. Tim laid down a Baby Ruth and Scotty picked out a Snickers from the rack beside the cash register. The man behind the counter rang up their purchases and handed them their candy.

"C'mon, Scotty," Tim said. "Lisa, put the comic book down. Come on."

I had been shadowing them even though Tim had repeatedly told me to go back home. Once we were out of the store Tim grabbed me by the arm and demanded, "Let me see what's in your pocket."

I tried to pull away but Scotty grabbed me by the other arm and Tim reached in my hip pocket and pulled out a bag of Sugar Babies. "Are you ever in trouble, Lisa!" Tim said.

Scotty added, "I'm going to tell Mom on you!"

"Why? It's just a little bag. You guys got to buy candy. How come I can't have any?" It just wasn't fair!

Timmy's prediction that I would get in trouble was accurate, but the punishment came from Guy, not Mom. He used the belt on me and I had bruises for days.

I tried stealing again not long after the first incident. I stole a water raft. There was a pool at a little apartment complex near our duplex and there was a little cut-through to go to the park in back of the complex. Every time

I cut through, I saw a raft hanging on the brick wall. What I expected to do with it I don't know, but I wanted it. Besides, other people had a raft. Why couldn't I have a raft? I pulled it off the hooks and started running.

My brothers told on me again but this time it was my tired mother who punished me. She hit me so hard on my upper legs with a hair brush that the bristles left punctures on my skin. I never stole again after that.

Tim and Scotty hung together—but as for me, I was just a little tagalong, not only cramping their style but also being a nuisance to them. One day they both held me down while Scotty stuffed dog poop into my mouth. I know, boys will be boys . . . but I went into the house crying. Mom wasn't home but Guy was, and nothing happened to my brothers. Another time, my brothers locked me outside at night in the cold snow. I knew Guy had to be awake. They all just left me out there. So I crawled through a window and figured out how to get back inside. I could hear them laughing. That was not the only night that I felt like nobody really wanted me.

I had to find out about everything important on my own. I started my period when I was eleven and Mom didn't even find out until I was fifteen. We were on the reduced lunch program and I got $7 a week to cover the cost of my lunches. I almost never spent it on food at school. I used the $7 to buy myself something new or I used it to buy my female products. Every so often I'd eat. I was skinny. I ate a lot when I ate, but I skipped meals at school, not because I thought I was fat but because I either wanted something I knew no one would buy for me, or I needed something I was afraid to ask for.

If I were to summarize those years in Tulsa in one phrase, this would be it: lack of opportunities. I'm not sure I would have used that phrase then, and I'm almost certain my mom would have good and valid reasons to disagree with me, but almost every memory I have about those years centers on something I didn't get to do or wasn't able to have. My mom did the best she could, but back then all three of us children often felt "we don't have the money" was an excuse. Now I can see that it was more than that—we really didn't have the money.

There was one thing I did get to do, though: From the time I was about eleven, Mom put me on a plane to New Hampshire, about a two-hour drive from Southie, and I spent two weeks in the summer with Nana Frances and Papa Vinny Zerveskes. She didn't go—her fear of somehow running into Tommy in his part of the world was always real. Guy wanted to steer clear of New England, too. My brothers didn't often go, either—they didn't care much for going to an old cottage house so far away from their friends, I guess, but I sure did.

There was one time we all did go together to the New Hampshire cottage. I was about ten, probably the summer before I started flying there by myself. Scotty would have been thirteen, Tim sixteen. We had flown from Oklahoma. This is the first plane ride I remember. When we were ready to go back to Oklahoma, Papa and Nana gave us their car, as they were planning to buy a new one.

I remember a lot about that visit. I served Papa ice cold Coors beers. I got real good at pouring them into frosted glasses with the perfect buildup of foam, just the way he showed me. Since Papa owned and worked at the Columbus Tavern, he was real good at pouring beers just right and coached me on how to do it. We cooked out, went paddle boating, and played cards and board games. Papa went for walks every day and sometimes I would go with him. Mom and I went into town shopping with Nana.

On the way home in our new car we stopped one evening in a small town. "Mom, there's a movie theater a few blocks down! Can we go?" Tim did the asking.

"Okay, but you have to take Lisa. We'll just stay here and rest."

The three of us went off alone. The movie was either *Night of the Living Dead* or *Pet Cemetery,* something that scared me very much. After the lights came on my brothers seemed to have disappeared. I was left by myself. They left me there. I had to find my way back to the motel in a strange town in the dark and after watching a scary movie. I had no idea how to find the motel, but somehow I did. For a ten year old, I was already pretty good at navigating my way around, and I suppose a guardian angel had been assigned to watch over me since I was left on my own so many times.

Nobody came looking for me. When I pounded on the door, Tim opened it. "Where were you?" he asked. Obviously he knew where I had been. I told Mom and Guy what had happened. I remember Tim and Scotty did get in trouble for that. But I don't remember who punished them or how.

After that trip, I started to fly to New England alone. Nana would pick me up because Papa never learned to drive a car. Papa's and Nana's waterfront cottage was on Sunset Lake in Farmington, New Hampshire. I got to do things there that I would have never even dreamed of in Tulsa. I swam a lot, played cards with my grandparents and their friends, ate good food, and helped my grandmother cook and clean up. The cottage was rustic, probably only about 900 square feet, with an open room including the kitchen and living area and two bedrooms. A windowed porch ran the width of it, and I loved opening and closing the jalousie windows each day. A paddle boat sat on the shore and there was a canoe in the basement we could carry out. Before Papa's walks, Nana would chase Papa around the cottage with a bottle of sunscreen, putting it on his face, his neck, and his arms. He would always push her away, saying, "Enough is enough, Jesus Christ, Frances, leave me alone!"

My cousin, Troy, who was a couple of years younger than I, often came and stayed a few days while I was there, and we also drove to visit Uncle Vinny and Aunt Sharon, Troy's parents, at the motel they owned, where Papa, Nana, and I stayed in a room on their property. My aunt and uncle loved eating fancy foods like lobster and steamers, and I grew to love them, too. Lobsters especially—I always looked forward to having at least two or three on every summer stay there.

There is one side trip that was not a part of those summer stays: trips back into Southie. Nana told me that they were afraid of what my father might do if he got word somehow through the neighborhood grapevine that she and Papa had me with them. I remember going there only two times, and they were short trips of necessity. We stopped at the bank and then at Papa's and Nana's three-story house only for an hour or two so Papa could pick up some mail and tend to some important things, and then we immediately got in the car and drove back to Sunset Lake. Not exactly time to forge a connection there. Yet I did look at the men walking on the streets and wonder, is he my dad? Does he know my dad? What does my dad look like now? Why is my mother so afraid?

The questions didn't consume me, but they were there, as maybe they also are in the minds of others like me who want to complete their family puzzle. Years would pass before I'd fit some of those pieces into the portrait of Lisa Connors.

Sleepovers, 1980s and 1990s

"Do you want to spend the night?"

"Sure." I knew my mom wouldn't care—she probably wouldn't even know. Trisha had a big family, a fun family. I liked staying there.

We did the usual stuff that evening. We listened to a new album, had dinner together, ate some popcorn, and then went to bed in her room. Her sister Meredith cleared out and slept on the couch so I could have her bed.

We talked quite a while, giggling, sharing our latest secret loves, before I realized Trisha's breathing sounded really regular. I turned over and fell asleep, too.

Well, almost. I slowly roused myself, realizing there was someone lying next to me. He had put his hand under my t-shirt.

"Get off me!" I whispered. I shoved him as hard as I could. "Get out of here!" At first he didn't move but I pushed him harder.

"Okay. Keep your voice down." The person grabbed onto the wooden bedpost to keep from falling. Though it was dark, I knew who it was. It was Trisha's Uncle Paul.

Though I kept what had almost happened to myself, after that I didn't spend the night at Trisha's house anymore. She and I were together, though, one day after school when she said she needed to stop at her aunt's to pick up her mom's purse, which was supposed to be on the front hall table.

The door was open so we went in. "Shhh!" Trisha whispered. "Do you hear that?"

I did hear something—a grunt, or maybe two. Trisha put her finger to her mouth and we tiptoed toward the room it was coming from.

The door was closed, but it had one of those old-fashioned keyholes you could peek through. And what we saw was an eyeful. Trish's sister Meredith was under their uncle Paul, who was moving back and forth over her. Her jeans were down, her shirt up. His jeans were on the floor. Meredith's eyes were closed and her hips were moving in time with his.

Meredith was thirteen, Trisha and I twelve. We grabbed the purse and got out of the house. We didn't say much to each other on the way home, but Trisha did ask, "I wonder if I should tell my mom?"

I didn't know how to answer her. How do you tell your mom that her brother is having sex with your sister? Since I stopped staying at Meredith and Trish's after that, I started gravitating to another house, the Demaros', where I spent nights and sometimes weeks at a time with my friend's family.

* * * * *

How a year or two can change things. I was fourteen when I began to spend the night at a different kind of sleepover.

"I'll be sleeping over at Allie's tonight. When Mom comes home tell her I'll be back in time to catch up on the wash tomorrow morning. We're going to go the game and then she's having a slumber party." Guy barely nodded. His eyes were closed as he lay on the couch, listening to the driving beat of ZZ Top's album *Eliminator*.

It was a convincing lie, and one I had used before. Allie hadn't invited me to her house that Friday evening and I'm sure she had no idea I was using her as my excuse to meet Tony down the street from the bar where he worked. I'd be sitting in a booth during his working hours nursing a drink and afterwards we'd go to his place.

Tony was waiting for me. "Hey, Lisa. Hang onto this." He handed me a driver's license. The girl in the picture looked like me if you didn't look at it too closely. "Jennifer Wilbrowski, birth date 01/04/66." That would make her twenty-one, not fourteen, which I was.

I had my mother's tall blond looks, including her legendary "caterpillar eyebrows," a distinctive family trait that marked my mom's brother Vinny's kids and us three kids as cousins. As with nearly everything else about me, I hated them. But for some reason my looks, eyebrows notwithstanding, seemed to be more than okay with the boys in the neighborhood. It was funny, because I was taller than a lot of them, almost five-feet-nine inches tall.

Tony was one of the older guys who had started hanging around me at Hillcrest Park, where I would meet up with some girls from school to drink and toke. Neither Guy nor my mother had any idea what I was doing. Mom was asleep during the daylight hours and gone during the nighttime hours. Guy was—well, I don't think he was doing much other than reading his library books and listening to music. I also knew he was drinking a lot because he didn't hide the evidence very well. I wonder what my mother would have done had she known how I was spending my time after school. I had been doing some recreational drugs, mostly weed, for a couple years. I wasn't all that into pot, but it was something to do.

And I needed something to do. I needed something to keep me out of trouble and I didn't have it. The popular girls at school seemed to like me and they invited me to go to the movies or bowling or whatever they were doing that weekend with them, but I didn't have the money to participate in the things they did. Some of them were cheerleaders and I wanted to cheer, too, and I was told, "There's not enough money." I really wanted to play basketball and I was told, "There's not enough money." More than cheerleading or basketball, I really, really wanted to play volleyball. I even went to practices to observe the other kids play. I asked for a lot of things but eventually I stopped asking. It's possible I didn't even ask about volleyball.

Never enough money. The only time any of the three of us participated in a school activity was one season in which Scotty was allowed to wrestle. Never enough money for us to be involved in extracurricular activities.

Never enough money—and yet I noticed there was always enough money for Mom and Guy to go out. That sounds like sour grapes, I know. But I knew there also seemed to be enough money for Guy to buy the booze that he thought he was drinking on the sly. Did Mom know how much he was drinking? Did she close her eyes in more than just a literal sense when she came home and went to sleep during the day? Maybe she was too tired to deal with it. If she had known, would she have given us a different answer to our desire to be involved in school activities?

In any case, I found something else to do. I became sexually active. By the time I started using "Jennifer's" ID to get into the place where Tony worked, he and I were already sleeping together every weekend. I went to more "slumber parties" than probably any other girl in the school. The relationship lasted a year, and it was the precursor to a relationship with more lasting consequences. I'll relate that story soon.

But let's go back to Southie to find out what my dad was up to there as I became a teenager in Tulsa. While I was looking for love, so was my father. The ways we looked for love are surprisingly similar.

LOOKING FOR LOVE, 1980S

Today when I compare my dad's life in South Boston to my own life in Tulsa during my middle school and teen years, I realize something that surprises me: We were very much "like father-like daughter." Each of us attempted to satisfy our need for love in ways that were flawed, and we had to accept the consequences of settling for less.

We each filled the loneliness with relationships that were, at best, imitations of love. While I was passing for a woman old enough to drink and having sex with a man who could have been arrested for statutory rape at an age when I should have been playing varsity girls' basketball and going to school dances, Tommy was going from relationship to relationship, always insisting that his current lady not try to reel him in. Which is a pretty good way to put it, because when he wasn't boxing he was often fishing. John "Red" Shea, a young boxing protégé of Tommy's who would become a central figure in his life, describes my dad during those years:

> Tommy was, and is, a true character. Five foot five inches tall, a buzz of constant chatter and activity. Tattoos of striped bass on his arm and across his chest, a large belt buckle with a striped bass across the gut. He loved fishing as much as boxing. . . He also loved sex. . . [5]

He recognized that he was kind of a sex addict. He knew sex wasn't

---

[5] From *Rat Bastards: The Life and Times of South Boston's Most Honorable Irish Mobster* (New York: William, Morrow, 2002, p.30).

love, but it was fun and it would have to do, because he was not going to give his heart to anyone again. It was a matter of practicality, of survival, even.

When he had first admitted to himself that Judy and his three kids were probably not coming back, he had gotten a little out of control. He had recently landed a job at City Hospital as a maintenance man and he was barely able to get through the days. He couldn't eat, couldn't sleep.

His brother Jimmy had met him at the Shamrock for a burger after work one day and watched his little brother take a couple bites and then put it down in disgust. "For the love o' God, Tom, you gotta get hold o' yourself!" Jimmy put his arm around Tommy's shoulder and said, "Let's go see my lawyer. He'll know what you can do to get her back."

What Jimmy's lawyer told Tommy was not what either Jimmy or Tommy had expected to hear. Tommy's version of the advice goes this way:

I've seen the strongest, smartest men in the world die, or turn into drunks, drug addicts, it's hopeless! You can't go after her, you gotta let her go. That's the only way you can survive. Let her go. They will come back, one day they'll come back. They will come back, not you, they—the children, or a child. One of those children will track you down. Most likely it will be the daughter, 'cause they're the most inquisitive or curious.

Tommy took the lawyer's word to heart. He told the women he hooked up with, "This is fun. No love. Got it?" Yet he pulled out everything in his bag of tricks to please them. He tried to play the field, though he did get into what he thought of as "no strings" relationships with more than one woman. However, sometimes the women didn't quite see the relationship the same way he did.

One relationship started about six months after my mom, my brothers, and I disappeared. It started out as a professional relationship with the psychiatrist who tested him and diagnosed dyslexia as the reason he never learned to read well, but before long the relationship turned physical. A friend of his, a former pro fighter, was an orthopedic surgeon, at the hospital where Tommy worked in the kitchen. He took Tommy aside one day and said, "Tommy, you're really screwed up. I'm going to take care of the first few sessions for you with a psychiatrist friend of mine."

That's how he met the beautiful, exotic-looking brunette psychiatrist, Helen. Ever the talker, Tommy describes what happened:

I let it go . . . and she says, "Well, I can see, you're a little nuts." But here's the thing: before long she was asking me about all these odd sexual things she had always wanted to do and I loved to do. So I threw it on heavy. I embellished it.

We started going out. She liked what she saw. I'm in a weakened state. And she started using it. And I said, "Honey, I may say 'I love you' at certain times and so on. But I'm not looking for love when my mind's gone [somewhere else]. I don't want children. I don't want to get married, you know? I can see being happy with you. But I don't want to lie to myself. I don't want to hurt you."

And uh, I says, "I hope you're taking contraceptives."

She says, "Oh, don't worry, Tommy. I am, every day, every day, every day." And then I started going over there three, four, five days a week. So all of a sudden she says, "Tommy, I'm pregnant."

I says, "You shouldn't have said that to me."

And I was gone. . . I hated to be cold, but wow!

About a year and a half later, I see her walking down the boulevard. She's got a baby boy in a carriage. I park the car and get out to say "hi" and she tells me she's married a detective and that he's abusive, a drunk and co-caine user.

I says to her, "Jeez, I know you're a nice person. You don't deserve that shit. You couldn't figure that out before you married him?"

I smile at the baby and ask how old he is, and she says something I didn't pick up on until I drove away.

I smiled at the little guy in the carriage and she goes, "He's ten months old. He's got a big head just like his father."

And I said, "Okay, Congratulations to him." Later on, I'm saying to myself, why would she say that to me? I mean, I've got kind of a big head for a little guy. So, I have no idea. She never called, never said nothing. So I actually thought, you know, there was no problem. I thought she got rid of it.

She never called me. She had my phone number. She knew I was at the gym.

A couple years later I saw Helen's mother and she told me her daughter had left the abusive husband, had married again, and was doing well.

That's the last time I heard anything about Helen. But I tell ya, that was the closest time I ever came to getting crazy over anyone. But you gotta remember, I was in a very weakened state.

I usually don't deal with girls, because I train men. But if I was dealing with [advising a girl about relationships] a girl, I'd give it to her straight up. 'Cause why lie? Why hurt anyone? When you're in that state of mind, just have a relationship and do what I do. Tell 'em straight up front. "I only want a relationship." If you think it's turning into more than that, walk when ya wanna walk.

Positively. Positively. But I broke it off. You know? I kept saying, "Honey, honey, honey, honey." You know, I was getting stronger, she was getting weaker. "I don't want to hurt you," I says. "We can be happy, but I got to be strong before I make that final commitment. So don't you make it."

During the 1980s, Tommy's ability to genuinely love and commit himself to a woman seemed lost forever. He missed his kids and wondered if they missed him. He wasn't sure what to do with his life. He knew as a school dropout his career options were limited. He tried becoming a barber and was good at the trade, but his reading skills were so poor he failed the written part of the certifying exam.

As he began to pass his own prime as a boxer, he turned to mentoring boys in the art, teaching classes out of some of the local gyms. From time to time he also taught self-defense to women. He took training others seriously and had a knack for picking out the boys who had talent to go pro as he had.

He burned off a lot of energy those ways, but his appetite for sex needed satisfying, and he got it satisfied—there were plenty of willing partners and his talkativeness charmed them.

Several years later, he did have another relationship that he is reluctant to talk about. The details remain with him, but I do know that a child resulted from the relationship, a girl.

Now I return to the red dirt of Oklahoma, where the wind comes sweepin' down the plain.

A New Start in Southside, 1980s

It all started out so well. We were moving. The house was in a neighborhood that local people call "Southside." After being crowded into a one-bedroom duplex for more than ten years, I was going to get my own bedroom. It had pink flowery wallpaper and my mom promised me one of those pretty white day beds that many of my friends had. Bless Nana and Papa—Papa had sold his tavern and had sent Mom $10,000 for this new start.

Then my mother's health problems happened very quickly. She had to have a hysterectomy, and she developed complications that landed her immediately in intensive care. At one point during her time in the recovery room she quit breathing for several seconds and the attending physician had to use the paddles to restart her heart.

I wanted to see, I needed to see, my mother. Yet the hospital had a policy of not letting children into intensive care. So Guy and I finished the move into the new home by ourselves so at least Mom would have a couch to lie on when she was released from the hospital. My brothers weren't around to help—Tim was away at Oklahoma State University and Scotty, well, he was in and out of the house, spending most of his time with his friends.

Finally the staff allowed me in to visit my mother, and seeing how weak she looked made my anxiety for her even worse. The next day Guy drove me to my new school and dropped me off. I went in to my first class and just sat there and cried. I couldn't shake the thought that my mother was dying and I was not there with her.

"What's wrong with her?" I heard the whispers and snickers as my classmates craned their necks backward to look at me. I got up and ran out of the classroom and out of the school. I knew how to get to the hospital and I ran all the way there to be with my mom.

"Please, let me stay here," I begged the wing receptionist. Since my mom worked there, one of the nurses bent the rules and allowed me to sit in the room next to my mom's bed. Some of the employees knew who I was and offered me some snacks, Jell-o, and juice.

I was more than glad to take them—we had no food in the house and I had no money to buy any. No wonder. It was obvious Guy was spending most of it on booze. It was obvious he was still drinking heavily—his bleary eyes and sluggishness gave him away. Please, someone, let some food appear in the cupboards, I thought. But none did.

My mother's best friend, Linda, head nurse on the hospital wing where my mom worked, called the next morning to check up on me. "Do you have anything to eat?" She asked.

"No. There's some spaghetti but no sauce and nothing else," I told her. "I asked Guy to bring home some groceries, but he didn't." Next thing I knew she was at the door holding a bucket of Kentucky Fried Chicken and all the fixings. She also brought in a bag of crackers, peanut butter and jelly, bread, sodas, and enough other items to completely stock the cabinets and refrigerator. When I look back at what Linda did for me that day, I realize the meaning of Christian charity. Talk about a friend in need.

The fact that Guy couldn't have a driver's license didn't keep him from driving. For several days he insisted on driving me to my new high school, me on the edge of the seat, afraid he'd have a seizure and not knowing whether I'd have to grab the wheel or what. He would pull up to the front and I'd walk in one door and out another. Then I'd run all the way to the hospital, about six miles. There I'd spend the entire day until Guy arrived in the late afternoon. He always smelled like a spilled drink of Jack Daniels mixed with sweat.

"C'mon, Lisa, you can't stay here all night. Let's go back to the house."

Not something I wanted to do, but Mom nodded weakly and said, "Lisa, go home," in agreement. This ritual became a pattern. Once we got home it didn't take him long to leave me there.

"Back in a few," he'd say, and he was gone, though not for long, and carrying a six-pack or fifth of whiskey when he returned.

Neither Guy nor Mom had a checking account as far as I knew. He had to be getting into Mom's money, I thought. I thought of that money as a fresh start and our future and he was drinking it away while my mom was in the hospital recovering from major surgery. I had to find it and hide it.

I opened the chest of drawers she kept her underwear in, fished around, and found it—a big wad of twenties and hundreds rubber-banded under her winter nightgown. I looked at it for a while. It was the most money I had ever seen.

I found the perfect spot to hide it—on the floor right behind the toilet. The toilet was close to the wall and the bathroom was dark. I put it in an envelope and stood back. I had to admit, it was nearly impossible to see it there. Later, when Guy came back in, he went to Mom's drawer. He started jerking the dresser drawers open and rifling through Mom's bras, panties, and sweaters. He found some change, picked it up, and threw it angrily on the floor, where it clinked against the wood before some of it rolled under the bed.

"Lisa! Lisa, where in the hell is the money?"

The anger in his tone scared me. I closed my bedroom door and locked it. Guy turned the doorknob quickly back and forth, back and forth, back and forth.

"Dammit, Lisa!" Then whump! Whump! He started slamming his shoulder against it. I did something I had seen in the movies. I grabbed a wooden desk chair and wedged it under the doorknob.

"Goddammit, Lisa, let me in!" Guy's voice was a roar of rage. I picked up the phone that I had dragged into the room by its long cord earlier.

I dialed 911. "He's trying to break down the door and I'm afraid he's going to hurt me!" I told the dispatcher.

"Young lady, calm down and tell me where you are," said the woman on the phone. "Why is he threatening you? Where is he right now? What is your address?"

The thumps against the door continued. I put the phone down on the floor, trying to hold the door closed with the chair. I pushed against it as hard as I could just like I had seen in movies. I wasn't a girl who prayed, but I did then: "Please, God, don't let him come in."

The thumping and the yelling stopped. He rattled the doorknob one more time and then I heard the click-click of his cowboy boots on the hardwood floor as he walked down the hall away from the door. Maybe he had given up—but maybe he was just waiting for me to come out—I didn't have time to think about where he might be. I just had to get out of the house, and fast.

I opened my bedroom door and ran out the front door. I just ran. The neighborhood was still new to me and I wasn't sure where I was going. I didn't have any place to go. The streets were poorly lit and it was hard for me to see, and I was a little worried about being accosted by a street person, or worse, by Guy himself. I wanted to go to the hospital, but I was afraid to walk there in the dark alone.

The QuikTrip looked like a safe place to wait for a few minutes while I decided where to go. As I walked into the parking lot, a police officer got out of a parked squad car and approached me. "Are you Lisa?" he asked.

I didn't answer him. He said, "Your stepfather is not well. We're going to take you to the hospital so you can be close to your mom. The nurses there will look after you."

I had no choice but to get into the back of the police car. First we drove to our house. "You stay here. I don't want any confrontations," the officer said. He went inside to find some clothes for me while his partner stayed with me in the car.

Linda once again stepped in to help. One of the policemen went in with me up to the pediatric unit where my mom worked. Linda gave me a hug. "Lisa, you can sleep here tonight," she said.

She took me to a small room where there was a hospital bed made up. As I think today of how she had that room made up for me, I don't know how she was able to pull that off, but it was such a relief to know I had a place to stay that I wanted to cry, and I did, a little, after she left the room. It was comforting to know I was on the floor my mom worked in, the pediatric unit. Throughout the night I could hear small children whimpering. "You want your mommy, and I know how you feel," I thought.

Next morning someone on the floor called the school to say I was at the hospital with my mother. She was doing better and a nurse's aide moved her out of intensive care into the room where I had slept the night before. I stayed with her the rest of the time she remained in the hospital as she was on the mend. Linda made arrangements for a visiting nurse to come to tend to her stitches and wounds and she was able to go home in a couple of days.

. . .To a quiet and empty house. She came in leaning on Linda's arm and I helped her over to the couch. "Here, Mom, here's your pillow," I said, scooting it under her head. She closed her eyes.

"I'll go see where Guy is," I said. But there were no boots or leather jacket to be found. It appeared he had gone. I felt sick until I looked behind the toilet. There the money lay, still hidden—still there. Well, at least Mom had her money. I brought the wad out to her and told her I had hidden it from Guy. She stuffed it under the couch, and the next day I walked the mile or so to school. I knew I had no excuse to keep me from going anymore.

The rest of the school week was relatively routine. The kids snickered at me in class. I guess they remembered me crying on my first day of school and that gave them a reason to laugh at me. I kept to myself. The nurses were coming to the house daily. Mom was still spending much of her days on the couch but she was starting to get up and do a few light chores. I was reluctantly going to school, but at least I was going.

On Friday, I walked into the house, feeling good. I was going to see a friend later. Mom was well enough for me to go to a Friday night "slumber party at Tammy's house," a lie that came easily to me.

I heard the shower running as I came in the front door. Mom spoke quietly. "Lisa, he's back. And you're not ever to say another word about this."

So that was that.

Guy and I didn't have much to say to each other after he came back, and my mom and I didn't, either. He seemed to really resent me. He didn't abuse me verbally, physically, or sexually, but he never spoke to me unless he had to, and I avoided him. We were through pretending.

Guy wasn't my father, and it was obvious he didn't want to be. We were in a bigger house and a nicer neighborhood, but our house was not really a home. I started making friends at the new school and began spending time with them, or I spent time with boys. I also smoked some pot and, well, did some other things, too.

"We'll Work Something Out," 1989

For the first time in my life I felt halfway pretty. Nana had come to Oklahoma for a visit and had given my mother money for me to get my chipped teeth fixed. My two front teeth had been chipped for almost eight years. I examined myself in the mirror. I saw a tall, thin girl. She had eyebrows that reminded me of furry brown caterpillars inching themselves along her forehead, and long and somewhat straight dark blonde hair—but she had a nice smile. "Lisa, you have to stop putting your hand in front of your mouth all the time," I ordered myself. It would take a while to get over the habit.

Dewayne and I had quite a relationship going. I had met him at the park as I hung around with my new friends. Whenever we got together we'd eventually end up at one of my friend's houses. Her parents worked during the day so we could be alone there. We weren't particular about where. As Bob Seger's song says, "We were just young and restless and bored."

Like me, Dewayne didn't have much of a family life. His penniless parents had left him in the care of an uncle who didn't seem to care much what he did. We were a matched pair, an accident waiting to happen.

I went to school only because I had to. I had a lot of trouble with reading comprehension, and, from time to time, I was labeled "special education," but I guess my problems didn't stand out all that much because somehow I kept getting promoted to the next grade.

We had no books in the house at all. Other than reading some in school, I don't recall ever reading a book at home. I don't recall ever owning one until I had my own money. My one attempt at trying to do a well-written and researched book report had been a failure.

The assignment was to read a famous person's biography and report on him. Of all people to choose, I chose Adolf Hitler. My reasoning was, there's gotta be something good about the man. Well, as I read the book, I realized there wasn't. I stood up in front of the class to give my oral summary but I couldn't finish it. I was mortified, and I ran out of the room. I didn't return that day, and the next day I found out I had received a "D." So much for trying.

So, I sat bored in the classroom, mind blank and with an attitude toward education that was simply not to make waves. I wasn't really noticed by the teachers as I sat thinking about what I'd be doing after school each day. I went to the nurse a couple times with what felt like the flu and she sent me home. Then I passed out in science class. An assistant principal escorted me to the nurse's office.

"Lisa, when did you have your last period?" she asked.

"I can't remember. It's been awhile. Why?" I answered.

She picked up the phone. After several rings my mother answered sleepily.

"Is this Lisa's mother? Would you please come up to the school? I need to talk to you about your daughter."

An hour later my mother was in the front office. The nurse, Mrs. Harrison, went to meet and talk with her a few minutes while I sat in the nurse's office drinking a small cup of 7-UP.

"Lisa, how in the world did you get yourself in this situation?" Mom asked as soon as Mrs. Harrison closed the door. I honestly didn't know. At first I didn't even completely understand her question. What situation? I was only fifteen. For someone who was sexually active, I was surprisingly ignorant. Consequences? No one had pointed out to me what would very likely happen if I kept sleeping around. At the age of fifteen, I wasn't the kind of girl who spent a lot of time thinking about my future, but I knew right away big changes were coming. Oh, God, for now just help me get over feeling like I need to throw up, I thought.

Mrs. Harrison explained the alternatives available for me through the Tulsa school system. "We will enroll Lisa in the Margaret Hudson Program, so she can be with other girls in similar predicaments. She can finish her high school education there and her diploma will list Edison High School as her place of graduation. I think this is best for Lisa, and, in fact, district policy does not allow unwed mothers here to mix in with the other students. It sets a bad example. Lisa, you'll do fine there. Let's get you back into class today and we'll set up an appointment for you there tomorrow. Mrs. Glaser, here's the name of a clinic that has had experience with unwed mothers."

Mom made me an appointment with the clinic, which confirmed the pregnancy. I was scared. I was self-conscious about the examination. I had almost no experience with doctors and I was embarrassed about having to take my clothes off in front of a strange man. I was frightened about labor and what it would be like. Most of all, though, two things bothered me: I was afraid I wouldn't be a good mother and afraid I wouldn't be able to provide nice things for my baby.

Mom wasn't very sympathetic about my condition. She began a campaign to get me to terminate the pregnancy.

"I think we should figure out how to get you an abortion," my mother said when the nurse called her into the examination room. I still had the blue-flowered wraparound gown on. I was having some cramps where the doctor had inserted the speculum. It had been so humiliating.

The gynecologist knocked softly on the door and came back in. "Let me give you some literature about alternatives," he said, handing my mother several pamphlets.

When we got home, Guy followed my mother into their bedroom. Sprawled across my pink bedspread, I could hear their soft voices. Guy went into the living room and switched on the TV. I grabbed my purse and my jacket and announced, "I'll be back soon." He looked at me but said nothing.

From the pay phone at the QuikTrip I called Dewayne. "I have to talk to you," I told him. He said he'd meet me in the park on his break from his job at Burger King. What was I going to do? I couldn't even get my mind around what the future held. I sat on a swing, my feet pushing me aimlessly back and forth through the hardened mud underneath the seat. He sat down on the swing next to me.

"My aunt had an abortion. I'll find out the name of her doctor," he told me. "She came through it just fine. We'll work something out, Okay? I better get back."

We'd work something out. I got up and walked back to the house, thinking about what that "something" would be. I already had decided I was going to have the baby, but I didn't know how. Mom's car was gone and I knew she had left for work. The TV had been turned off and I didn't know if Guy was there or not.

He wasn't. He had disappeared once again.

Mazzio's Pizza and Oprah

Guy was on the other end of the phone line talking with my mother. A week or so had passed since he had left.

He must have been calling from a pay phone in a busy place such as a bus station, because he was talking loudly as if trying to be heard over a lot of background noise and I could hear most of what he said. "I'm in Burlington, Vermont. I'm not ready to be a grandfather. If you want to move here, I will send money for you to move."

Mom answered him. "Well, I'd like Lisa to come with me."

And he said again, "I'm not ready to be a grandfather. You can't come with Lisa."

"Guy, I can't leave Lisa," she said.

So Mom stayed in Oklahoma. She and Guy got a divorce after eleven years of marriage and it wasn't long after that one of his cousins called to tell her that Guy had died while having a seizure.

I look back at a pregnant teenager and her mother who did the right thing, and I will be forever thankful for that sacrifice. I told Mom I was going to have the baby. By whatever the means, I'd make it work. My mother quit arguing with me about it.

There were some questions I had to answer, though: How would I manage? And how would I get through school? I didn't look obviously pregnant for quite a while, so I had a little time before I absolutely had to leave Edison High School and transfer to Margaret Hudson, the alternative school for pregnant girls. At least I wouldn't have to drop out of school—but I desperately needed money. I was fifteen but I looked older, so I applied for a job at Mazzio's Pizza nearby. The manager told me to come back when I was sixteen, so I did, as soon as I had my sixteenth birthday.

As it turned out, I worked at Mazzio's for more than four years. I operated the cash register, did salad prep, washed dishes, made pizzas, cleaned bathrooms, whatever they needed me to do. My new focus became earning enough money to provide for the child that was on the way. Eventually I transferred to Margaret Hudson School, which I could attend from 7:30-11:30 and then go straight to work afterwards.

My job at Mazzio's was hard work—then again, what restaurant work is easy? The atmosphere was pleasant and I got along well with my coworkers and my customers. No one realized I was pregnant for quite a few months. And as the life inside me grew, something began to happen that surprised me. This tall sixteen -year-old who didn't think she was either pretty or smart began to have a "fan club" of sorts—I developed some regular customers. They came to the restaurant only when they knew I'd be there. Even more surprising, several of them seemed to think I was both pretty and smart. That was new to me, and I liked it. I ate it up. Some of them even offered me jobs at other places like the phone company and other large corporations.

I also saw some opportunities to better myself a little. I was appointed a shift leader. As I proved my reliability and work ethic, I went to my boss and said, "Your turnaround is very high. There are always new people coming in and some are not very trustworthy." And I asked him for fifty cents per hour raise. He eventually gave it to me. "You're now the highest paid person in this restaurant," he told me. Meanwhile Ken, CEO of the company that owned Mazzio's and some other restaurants, stopped by the restaurant periodically, though I didn't know who he was. He came back again and observed me, though I didn't know he was watching me.

Something else had also begun to happen that surprised me at first. Maybe it started earlier, but it grew inside me as the baby did. As day after day I filled root beer mugs and carried steaming pizzas on metal trays to the red-and-white checkered oilcloth covered tables, I became convinced that I had to have an education.

Where did this certainty come from? I'm not completely sure why I became so intent on going to college. In some ways I have to credit Oprah. I watched her program on the days when I wasn't on the work schedule and I not only witnessed people who had jumped over hurdles that were higher than mine, but also became familiar with Oprah's own story. The sexual abuse she endured, her weight problems, her race—if she could be successful in overcoming those challenges, what was stopping me? She never gave up on reaching her goals, and that was a powerful example to me.

My new goal became to receive an education so I'd be a good role model for my child. I wanted my child to grow up in a different world than I had experienced. I felt it was time to get an education—because I did not want to be stuck on that self-defeating merry-go-round of teen pregnancy, welfare, ignorance, and poverty that I had seen so much of already. I wanted to take a flying leap off of it, and I believed education was the key.

Something else began to surprise me: As the months passed, I grew to feel pretty ready to have a baby. Dewayne didn't come around much anymore, but I didn't need him. With or without Dewayne, things were going to be different for my baby than they had been for my mother and for me.

Welcome, Zackery, Easter Sunday, April 15, 1990

"Lisa, it's okay. You're fine. You have a new baby boy. Look at him. He's beautiful."

Uh . . . who . . . I wasn't sure at first who was saying such a thing. It didn't register in my fogged brain. The room seemed as big as a gymnasium to me and the voice seemed to be coming from its opposite end.

"Mom? Mom?" I barely got the words out but they seemed to echo in the cavernous room.

The voice was Linda's. As a nurse at St. Johns where my mom worked and due to the relationships she had at Osteopathic Hospital, she got approval to come into the delivery room with me. She saw me grimace as I felt an uncomfortable pull between my legs, like someone was sewing right into my skin. "The doctor is doing an episiotomy," she explained. "You'll heal easier. He'll be done in a minute."

The doctor, a resident OB/Gyn at the hospital, looked up, smiled, and gave me a thumbs-up. "You're doing great, Lisa," he said. "Hang in there."

I roused myself enough to see that my legs were in stirrups and that the sheet draped over my legs was bloody.

"What happened, Linda? Where's my baby?"

"Lisa, honey, your baby boy is fine. See?" She motioned to the OB nurse, who smiled at me and brought me a squeaking, greasy little being. A clamped off cord was sticking out of his belly. She put him on top of my chest for a few seconds. "My God," I thought, "this came out of me?"

"He weighs 9 pounds 1ounce," she told me. "We'll let you hold him very soon. You're not quite up to it yet." She turned and handed the small bundle to another nurse in scrubs. "They'll take him to be cleaned up and put him under the lights. You can see him as soon as you're wheeled into a room."

Linda took my hand. "You had a pretty rough time of it going in and out of consciousness, but you're going to be just fine. As soon as they get you back in the room you can see that little boy. He looks just like you." That was a kind thing to say considering I had not seen Dewayne in weeks.

Turns out Linda was not exaggerating at all. I vaguely remembered someone holding my ankles, but I didn't know until she explained that I had had a couple of seizures while I was in labor.

I also didn't know until I was wheeled into a semi-private room on the maternity floor that I was still bleeding profusely. Linda stayed with the charge nurse, who sounded a little alarmed at the fact that my sheets were soaked. "I'm going to call the OB resident, STAT," she told Linda. "Can I talk to you a minute?" She motioned to Linda and they stepped out of the room for a minute, but I heard what she told her. "We may need to give her a bag or two."

By that time Mom was also in the room. She kissed me on the forehead. "Honey, you okay?" she asked. She didn't seem to expect an answer.

The OB/Gyn on duty came in followed by a technician carrying an IV pouch with a dark red, syrupy-looking something in it. The tech picked up my wrist, which already had a PIC line inserted in it, and said, "Now this will just take a minute."

"Oh no, she is not going to get blood. No way. Forget about it. There's too much risk." Linda again, quickly.

"But she has lost at least two quarts of blood and she really needs to replenish it," the doctor said. "I highly recommend at least a quart."

I had neither the energy nor the knowledge to agree or disagree with either of them. "She can replenish the blood if she drinks a lot of fluids," Linda argued. "Her mother does not want her getting some blood that might be tainted."

"That's right. God, no. No way in hell," Mom added.

So I didn't get blood. Later Linda told me she had fears about blood contamination due to the recent cases of AIDS-tainted donor blood. All I knew at the time was that I was tremendously thirsty, and keeping Linda's advice to keep drinking as much fluid, especially water, as I could was not hard.

I don't remember much about that first night in the hospital. I do remember seeing that red little face and holding that tiny human being. I peeked into the diaper at his little penis and scrotum, counted his fingers and toes, and thought, he's mine. He's my Zackery Ryan. I'm his mom. And he is so little. And what am I gonna do to support him?

After tentatively holding and feeding him for the first time I gave my son back to the nurse, who took him back to the newborn nursery. I drifted off into a light sleep. I dreamed that Dewayne was standing beside me. "Lisa, I came to see how you're doing," he told me in the dream.

Only it wasn't a dream. "Oh, hi, Dewayne," I mumbled. I think he told me he had seen the baby, but I was so groggy I didn't much care. He left a bouquet of carnations on my nightstand and left.

Within a couple days Zackery and I were at Mom's. With my earnings from Mazzio's I had bought some very nice baby items including a crib and a layette. I stayed there with her for about a year, and she really did help me out as much as she could and I helped her out, too, paying $50 each week for "rent." Scotty was in the house occasionally (more about him later), but Tim was already off to college, having gotten a scholarship and loans to get him through.

And so a new phase of my life began. Single mom, waitress, high school student. And only sixteen. Does that seem like a lot of responsibility to spoon onto a teenage girl's plate? It was. But the thing was, I had helped myself to those servings. I was having to swallow what I had heaped onto my plate and I just did what I had to do. Maybe it's good that my life had not been one of cheerleading, parties, dances, and school or church activities. My life had been, well, a life, and that's about it. So I didn't have to give up much.

And in fact, it became quickly evident to me that I had actually gained a lot more than I had given up. Zackery had the usual baby issues such as diaper rashes, spitting up and colic, and I quickly found out I would have no social life to speak of, but what new purpose he brought into my life. I saw him as both my gift and my responsibility, and I was determined to be a good mom.

MY FIRST REAL LOVE, ZACKERY

"Open your booklets. Use only a pencil. You can do your figuring in the margins. Let me repeat this: If you are caught cheating, you will automatically fail. Begin now." Passing the test meant that I would have just enough credits to graduate.

I had to take Oklahoma's state-mandated math test twice to get my high school diploma in 1991. That wasn't surprising, because I had almost no real education in mathematics. In view of the fact that I was virtually math illiterate the first score I got, 32 percent, was not so bad. I had two weeks to study, and I had to teach myself math, night after night, making every minute available of every day count. I read and learned and read and learned and tested myself and read and tested myself again. I figured the math out in two weeks—but doing so was very, very hard, and I was sleeping only a couple of hours each night.

The stress took its toll on my body. When I was a baby, I had contracted the cold sores virus, Herpes Simplex Virus (HSV). Often as a child and teenager I would have a flare-up caused from exhaustion or stress. However, never had I had a flare-up like I had during this time. Previously, I had had cold sores only on my lips. This time they spread all the way down to my chin. I was exhausted and looked it when I retook the exam, but I passed with a score of 82 percent. You do what you have to do. That had become my attitude.

Regardless of the quality of my education, with just enough credits, I graduated with an official high school diploma in 1991 that listed my school as Edison High School, not Margaret Hudson. Good education?

Bad education? It was a diploma, a means to an end. I was proud of the accomplishment.

Next up was the ACT. My score on it was only 14, barely high enough to enter Tulsa Community College. I started my first classes in fall of 1991. It's funny now to think how naïve I was about resources available to me. I knew of no financial aid programs or scholarships, so I paid my first two years of junior college myself. You do what you have to do.

I learned early on in Freshman Comp I that I was unable to even write a paragraph. I failed my first attempt at Freshman Comp I, and then my second. Finally, after repeating the course three times, I passed Freshman Comp I with an A. I finally turned in a paragraph that showed I "got it" about how to write something that was coherent. Writing about something I knew also helped. Here it is:

I still have that handwritten essay on lined notebook paper. At the bottom are these words: "Your paragraph conveys this [the instructor drew an arrow to "the joyous evening"] well! 20 points out of 20."

Then it was on to Freshman Comp II. I had to take it two times, but I ended up passing the second time with a B. A means to an end. . .

Zackery was sick a lot, mostly with ear infections. I always listened to everything the doctors said for me to do and I always asked a lot of questions. Eventually we put tubes in Zackery's ears. After that, his health was better, which helped me miss less school. However, whether I was missing more or less school, college was hard, for me, real hard.

Zackery went to day care when I went to my classes. My brother, Scotty, my mom, or my friend, Sherry, watched Zackery when I put in my one-night-per-week shift at Mazzio's. Money was tight, but not so tight that I couldn't put something away from each paycheck. I watched every penny, a habit that continues with me to this day. I don't think I learned the habit at home—while Mom always complained of not having enough money, I didn't see her doing anything special to save. Whatever the reason, I was bent on having a little stash for emergencies, if any came. I always felt something was lacking (and actually it was, wasn't it?) if I had nothing in my savings account.

This was a quiet time in my life considering all the responsibilities I had. I rarely even heard from Dewayne. At first, he dropped by with money and to see Zackery from time to time. Eventually, though, he stopped coming in, just leaving a little money in the mailbox. I had learned at Margaret Hudson how to force him to give me child support and I tried to follow through on that, but really, I knew I could manage without him.

When he stopped bringing money by to help out, I started through the process of taking him to court for child support. Apparently, the system was very backed up—it took about a year before the child support became official. Regardless, though, I decided that it would help me provide a better living for us and, looking back now, I believe it did.

Meanwhile Mike Still was continually encouraging me to make the best of myself and "my" customers at Mazzio's obviously liked me. My self-confidence was growing and I realized it was time to move into my own place. Mom had a new boyfriend, Dempsey. She was completely wrapped up in her new man. Scotty was in and out, sometimes gone for weeks, involved in things I figured out—namely, drugs. I felt like a fifth wheel. I knew it was time for me to make a step toward independence and a better atmosphere for Zackery and me.

By that time, I knew about "Section 8" housing, because some of the Margaret Hudson girls lived in the Section 8 projects. But I wanted more than that for Zackery and me. I worked hard and I could afford it. After all, I was the tightwad and thrifty spender. I found a little apartment on the south side of Tulsa right on the river, an area locals refer to as Riverside. We were only a short walk from bike trails, fishing, boating, arts and crafts, a café, picnic areas, and playgrounds. A perfect spot for us.

I was not interested in a long-term relationship with anyone because I was on a track that went toward one goal, and the wheels of my mind revolved continuously to the sound of "Get an education—get an education—get an education." It became my reason for being, other than my son, of course.

In spite of my single-mindedness, a couple of nice men came into my life. Neither one seemed bothered by the fact that he would have to compete with my studies, my job, and my motherhood responsibilities.

One of them, Jim, was quite a bit older than I. I dated him before Zackery was born and he came over a couple of times after Zackery's birth. He treated me fondly, and so did Shawn, a good man with whom I ended up in a two-year dating relationship. Gosh, Shawn was handsome. He looked just like actor Rob Lowe. And he seemed like a good person, but he didn't have a job and that was strange to me. His mother supported him and he lived with her. I often gave him gas money just so he could come see me.

When compared to the boys I had fooled around with before Zackery was born, each of these men was quite a few steps higher on the quality ladder, but I simply was not interested in getting serious. If I had been interested, I could have married Shawn, but I just couldn't do it. For one thing, he had much less ambition than I did, and also the timing was wrong. I had to break it off, not just for me but for Zackery, too.

I saw myself as having finally gotten my priorities straight, and looking back at what Lisa Connors was like during those years, I think I did. I told myself I didn't even have to have a boyfriend. I just focused on Zackery, reading to him and playing with him. Between Zackery, college, and work, I didn't have much free time. Or maybe I should say I didn't make much free time for myself, because opportunities to get into trouble were always fairly easy to find. During the little bit of free time I had, we enjoyed the simple pleasures that our apartment at Riverside offered us—fishing, picnicking, playing on the playground and simply sitting on a bench watching the birds and feeling the breeze off the river.

I was walking a pretty straight line. I was determined not to get myself into trouble and jeopardize my son's and my future. Or so I thought.

In some ways Zackery was my first real love. My love for him, and his love for me, changed my life for the better. "A little child shall lead them"––I'm no expert on the Bible, but that's in there somewhere, I think.

Where did my mom fit in during this time? She and Dempsey were seeing each other a lot and, other than spending time with him she continued working nights and sleeping days. Zackery and I would see her about once a week or so, when I would go help her by pumping gas in her car since she was so afraid of doing it herself. She was fearful of so many things, always looking behind her, always afraid Tommy was trying to find her after all the years we had been gone.

We heard nothing from him or about him, though. What is surprising to me now is that like my life, Tommy's life was about to change due to his love for a child. Next up, I'll follow the timeline back to Carson Beach so I can zero in on my dad and what was happening in his life.

Votes of Confidence from Surprising Places

I took Zackery with me to school in the mornings. The city school system provided day care at the alternative school during school hours, and then in the afternoon I dropped him off at a nearby day care center. On occasion a friend watched him if or when I worked an evening shift. It's amazing what a person can do when she has to or when she is determined to. Both of those "whens" were mine.

Margaret Hudson School was Tulsa's attempt to answer the dilemma of how to make sure pregnant moms and young mothers got their high school diplomas. My teacher friends tell me that if you walk down a public school hallway today, you're likely to see several pregnant girls who are integrated into the student population without a second thought, and they continue going to school up until the day they deliver in some cases. Not in 1989, though, at least not in Tulsa.

I look back at Margaret Hudson School with mixed, though, thankful feelings, because its existence meant that I could graduate high school, the first step toward my goal of getting an education. The facilities were pretty rudimentary—we didn't have textbooks, except for math textbooks. I don't recall learning much of anything there. It was the means to an end for me, as I think it was for most of the other girls there.

As I sit and look through the now faded pages of my senior yearbook, "1990-91 Memories," just a mimeographed collection of about fifteen pages held together with yarn, some memories float into my mind.

I turn to the photo of the senior graduates, class of '91, at the beginning. In the picture of the twenty smiling young women dressed in their Sunday best, someone is missing—me. Getting to work on time for the lunch shift was more important than getting my picture taken. I remember some of the girls—several had more than one child already, some were already married, others were "unwed mothers," like me. Racially and ethnically we were a mixed group, but we all had a common goal, and it was to get our high school diplomas. While Margaret Hudson was the school I attended, my 1991 diploma showed that I had graduated from Edison high school, where I had gone before I got pregnant. But I'm getting ahead of myself a little. . .

There is a picture of me in those faded pages and a statement of my "will," in which I offered my job "to anyone that wants it." In the photo, I am in shorts; I'm long-legged, slender, with long, thick, honey-blonde hair. I'm sitting on a jungle gym, smiling (thank God for Nana) and above the picture is the caption, "Most Likely to Succeed." What a vote of confidence- -apparently not only my smile but my attitude toward school had improved by that time.

Another boost in my confidence came from the restaurant. One after-noon a man came into Mazzio's from the company headquarters. He called me over to a table and asked me to sit down. "Lisa, we'd like for you to con-sider taking a job at our executive office," he said. The money he offered me was quite a bit more than I was making.

"I'll think about it," I told him. "Can I let you know?" It seemed like a great opportunity. Yet I was afraid that if I accepted the money and went to work there, I wouldn't have the opportunity to be educated. I continued to carry the confidence that education was the key to success, and by "success" I meant it was the tool to break out of the cycle of poverty and teen pregnancy.

So I hesitated in accepting the offer. One night soon after that, Mike Still, one of my regular customers, asked. "Lisa, can I talk to you after your shift?" He was a pleasant man who often came in with his two young children, a boy and a girl. I could predict their orders: Andrew, a sausage regular crust; Leah, a veggie pizza or Alfredo and sometimes a salad; Mike, always a salad and sometimes a pasta or thin crust pizza.

We met in the atrium at the front of the restaurant. He told me that he had a nanny that lived with them but the children weren't happy with her. "Leah and Andrew love you," he said. "You always have a smile on your face. I know it's not always easy to smile for someone who has all the responsibilities you do. To look at you, a person would never know that you've had all this adversity in your life. I would like to offer you a job helping out with my children and cleaning house. Of course that would mean some overnights, and you would be welcome to live at the house in the guest quarters, but you could go to school, whatever you need to do, during the day."

"So where do you live?" I asked. I was flabbergasted when he told me. "You mean the one with the swimming pool and tennis courts, the one where the big dogs chase you if you walk near the house?"

"Yes, that's the one. Why don't you think about it? You can also start out slowly, just babysitting for Leah and Andrew if you'd like."

"You mean I can have Zackery with me while I work?" I watched Mike as he drove away in a convertible Porsche. I was still surprised at how wealthy he appeared to be.

It made me feel very good that he was so interested in me. I tried staying with the kids and it worked out wonderfully. So . . . I didn't accept the job at headquarters. I began staying with nine-year-old Leah and five-year-old Andrew in the evenings and then eventually all night, taking Zackery with me. I also took a job offer Dewayne's aunt arranged at her work as a part-time file clerk for a chiropractic office. The hours were flexible, allowing me to work three hours one day, six hours another day, sometimes once a week or sometimes more, whatever fit into my school and work schedule and dependent on how much filing there was.

Mike became like a father to me in many ways. He worked for a small division of a major oil company that manufactured oil pumps. Later he brought me in to answer the phone and prepare shipping manifests and payroll, and I also learned some simple accounting. I loved it. I enjoyed the challenge of learning. It was a new world and I felt like it was opening some possibilities for me.

Leah and Andrew were great kids. Zackery and I fit into the Still family as if we were part of it. I stayed at Mike's often. Nannying for him was a perfect gig since I could take Zackery with me, and he had a good time being entertained by the older children. I also loved taking the kids skating, bowling, swimming, whatever we did, we had a great time.Mike paid me very fairly and often gave me bonuses. He was a good man, always a gentleman toward me and always encouraging me to be the best I could be. I always knew that he admired and respected me, and that meant a lot to me.

And I learned something from Mike, which might sound as if it should already have been obvious to me, but it wasn't. While he had plenty of money to buy the more expensive brands of food and dry goods, he bought the generic brands and he always looked for ways he could to economize. He'd tell me, "They're just as good, and they're cheaper." That was a good lesson in money management for a poor girl. I've never forgotten it, and I follow it to this day.

So . . . time to quit Mazzio's? I didn't see it that way. I loved the 50 percent discount I got on the food—and I could use coupons besides! More so, though, I loved my regular customers. So I worked Wednesday nights 6-9 p.m. As an employee I could take "my" kids, pick up a salad, and have a great, cheap meal for all four of us. So that's what we did. We had some nice little pizza parties, and a good time was had by all.

A FATHER FINDS A "SON," LATE 1980S

Tommy got personal satisfaction from mentoring the boys he took under his wing in South Boston's fight clubs and gymnasiums. Knowing he'd probably never be able to be a role model to his own two boys and his daughter and having a store of frustrated love that needed an outlet, he realized right away that when he helped the kids to stay out of trouble it made him feel better. He knew all too well how easy it was to let Southie be the winner in the struggle to making something of oneself. He wanted his protégés to figure out how to make Southie a tool rather than a barrier.

Once in a while Tommy trained someone who went on to be famous in one way or another. One of his most memorable trainees was Peter Welch, who later won a Golden Gloves Championship and became the trainer and coach for the *Ultimate Fighter* reality series on Spike TV, as well as an actor in movies such as *The Departed*.

Another of Tommy's trainees later got quite a reputation for his AIDS activism. Like Tommy, Jon Stuen-Parker was a product of the streets. He made a few wrong turns into drug addiction, which resulted in a two-year jail sentence. He eventually got his life together, graduated from Yale with a degree in public health, wrote a memoir called *Letter to Norman Mailer: From Jail to Yale* (National AIDS Brigade, 1998), and became a vocal and controversial advocate of free needles for addicts. His early promise as a boxer, though, was cut short by his drug use.

Jon was a colorful character even before he went straight. About six feet tall, 180 pounds, he was the perfect cruiserweight. He wore his long hair in a braid. Tommy didn't know Stuen-Parker was a heroin addict at that time. Heroin addiction was something Tommy would not tolerate in his trainees. If he had known that Jon was using, that would have been the end of their training sessions.

Tommy's reasons for not tolerating drunkenness or drug use were personal. He had seen the damage in his own family that addiction would cause. His brother Jimmy, who had both seen and experienced what drugs will do to a person while he was at Walpole, had warned Tommy years ago to steer clear of anyone, even if it was Jimmy himself, who wanted to stick a needle in his arm. He didn't have to do much to convince Tommy, because Jimmy himself was Exhibit A on the damage that drugs can do. Tommy saw heroin addicts in Southie who robbed their own families without even stopping to think about what they were doing.

He had also learned from personal experience about what can happen when a person drinks too much. One St. Patty's Day he was drinking wine, beer, and whiskey, really putting it away. He woke up with thirty stitches in his face and a broken front tooth. He couldn't remember how he got so banged up. "Did I do that, or didn't I do that?" he asked himself. He decided he didn't like not being in control. It was too dangerous.

Though he trained countless boys and a few girls over the years, Tommy rarely saw real raw boxing talent, but he did once in a while. Some of the Hispanic kids he mentored, in particular, often had the drive, the single-mindedness, and the brute strength to succeed. At bottom, though, it wasn't the race, ethnic group, body type, or size that made the difference between a good amateur boxer and a great one. It was rage, anger "busting" to get out, and to have something or someone to take it out on. Tommy recognized it, because it was like looking in a mirror.

So when he saw young, red-headed John Shea, he knew what he was looking at. There the kid was—a younger version of himself. Tommy took him under his wing and began to train him seriously and hard. The kid had the seeds of greatness in him. They were aching to have an outlet, and Tommy wanted to make sure they got it.

John "Red" Shea became Tommy's pride and joy. He took the place of the sons Tommy could not be close to, and, in turn, Red looked up to Tommy as a father figure.

Tommy explained later, "I trained him since he was five years old. I had a thing with this kid. He was like a baby brother. No, he was a son." He took the boy with him when he went fishing, which was his other great love when away from the ring and the gym.

In some ways young Red Shea was so like Tommy that his story was like Tommy's history repeating itself. Of Irish-American parentage like Tommy, Red had an alcoholic father who was long gone. He was the youngest child in the family as Tommy was. He had learning problems at school, as Tommy had had. He was small as a child, maybe not as small as Tommy had been, but small. He was poor. And he was full of rage, tired of being picked on by his mother, his three sisters, and his teachers.

In his memoir *Rat Bastards* (William Morrow, 2006), Shea explains his mentor Tommy's training approach: "hands up, jab, jab, step and hook, right to the body, uppercut, left hook, and move. Run, squat, work, lift the heavy bag. Eat right. Do a thousand pushups a day. Run, run, run, run, run (28). And when Tommy saw Red becoming interested in girls, he also taught him to stay away from sex in the days leading up to a fight. "That pent-up testosterone makes you stronger," he told the boy.

Under Tommy's training Red began his boxing career as a young child. He worked his way through Baby Golden Gloves competitions and boxed as a young teenager in some important bouts. He was on his way to a bright future as a young boxer.

When he hit his teens, though, Red's life outside the ring took some wrong turns, and Tommy may have been inadvertently responsible for one of them. Red was one of the Southie high school kids who the government in its all-knowing wisdom bussed into Roxbury, always a tough neighborhood and by then almost entirely black. His fists got the better of a couple of young toughs, which labeled him as Enemy # 1 on the gangs' lists. Tommy told him, "Kid, you're gonna end up being stabbed. You ain't learnin' nothin' up there. You're going to school to fight. You're gonna end up dead."[6]

Under Tommy's advice, Shea quit school in tenth grade. That gave him essentially nothing to do but train, box, and look for trouble. Which he found soon after. He and a couple friends took up a life of petty crime and harassment, shoplifting and so on. He got into a fight with a niece at one of his sisters' houses, which resulted in assault charges being filed. Good lawyering got him acquitted, but he was slip-sliding away. The slippery slope led to drug dealing, which he became very good at, developing some impressive math skills in learning to divvy up scores and profits.

---

[6]Shea's words quoting Tommy, 32.

He and Tommy remained very close. In fact, Tommy put Shea's name on a Florida property he had purchased. He knew by then that his "son" was dealing and several mutual acquaintances warned him not to do it, but he was family, wasn't he? Tommy had to have a back and neck operation and he figured if he died, the property should go to someone close to him.

That decision would come back to haunt him. Shea's name on that deed and some phone conversations between Tommy and Shea in the mid-to-late 1980s were eventually going to end up as evidence in a series of events that would not turn out well for either of them.

LEARNING ABOUT TOMMY, 1990–1991

I wonder if ignorance really is bliss. Ignorance can be defined a lot of ways. In my case, I thought of ignorance as lack of education. It did not occur to me that ignorance could also simply be lack of knowledge, or that often knowledge is, itself, an unwelcome thing. Maybe it is blissful to be ignorant after all.

In some ways it was for me. I was still going regularly to visit Nana and Papa at the cottage about once a year when my schedule would let me. After Zackery was born, I carried him on the plane with me. He got lots of attention from the extended Zerveskes family at the lakes. We'd strap a lifejacket on him and carry him to a shallow part of the lake, roll a beach ball with him, or show him crawdads and frogs.

I knew nothing of what was happening in Southie, though I was becoming more and more curious about my dad. I had the beginnings of a desire to show my little boy to my father. I didn't think my mother knew how to track him down, but even if she did, she wouldn't tell me. She still didn't go anywhere without looking over her shoulder, and if she left her car unattended, she would look in the back seat, keys in her hand, before she unlocked it and got in.

I remember a trip to New Hampshire around the year 1990 or 1991––I'm not sure if Zackery was born yet or not—when Nana told me she wanted to show me something. "Help yourself to some coffee," she said. "I'll be back in a minute."

I put a teaspoon of instant Sanka (ugh! but they liked it) in one of Nana's white ironstone cups and sipped it. Why in the world did they still use this awful concoction? They never made perked coffee. I laughed to myself at the habits they held to.

I heard the click of Nana's suitcase snapping shut. She came into the kitchen with a couple of newspaper clippings from the *Boston Herald* and *Boston Globe.* "You asked me if I knew anything about your father and if I knew anything about him. Here's something about him in the paper."

So the guy being arrested for drug-dealing was my *father?* What was I supposed to think?

"This is really something, Nana."

"Yes. Maybe they'll finally put him behind bars," Nana said without a trace of sympathy or sorrow that she had shown me such damning information about my father. "And they'll also put that scum James Bulger in jail," she said. "And him with a brother in politics!"[7]

Papa walked in and took a bottle of Moxie and a half gallon of milk out of the refrigerator. ("Moxie" is hard to describe. It's an old New England soft drink with a "unique" taste—some would say "medicinal," while others might compare it to cream soda, and many might just say "awful." It's often drunk with milk and some people are convinced it has curative qualities.) Papa poured Moxie halfway to the top of a glass and added milk to the rest. "He's no goddamn good. Maybe now his crooked shenanigans will come back to bite him in the ass," he said.

Papa had a way of saying things that made me smile in spite of my-

---

[7]James "Whitey" Bulger's brother, Billy chose politics as a way of making a name for himself. He went into local politics at first, later becoming the president of the Massachusetts Senate and the president of the University of Massachusetts. He has been controversial. Rumors have circulated about his connections with his brother's activities from time to time. As Whitey is put on trial, perhaps some of these rumors will resurface.

self. He and Nana often were like an Archie and Edith Bunker with Boston accents. Papa had an opinion on every subject—never mind if it was informed or not. He and Nana would go at each other sometimes, with Nana goading him and Papa muttering, "Yeah, yeah, yeah, get off my back." Or he'd end an argument by walking out of the room and saying, "You'll drive me out of my god . . . damn . . . mind." Or he'd pick at Nana and she'd bristle and say, "Whaddaya want from me?" But they were like two sides of the same coin. They went to Mass together at the parish down the street every Sunday, and they always treated me with love.

I sat there sipping that god-awful instant coffee, silent, but thinking, so now I have a brother who I am pretty sure is using drugs and a drug dealer for a father. Sad.

Yet seeing my dad's name in the paper made me wonder a little about how he had gotten into that kind of trouble and what kind of person he was. Nana and Papa told me about the big sting operation that had jabbed at South Boston's not-so-hidden underbelly of drug-related crimes and murders. They said people in Southie talked about how Tommy ran drugs to Florida. Supposedly, that was his connection to the whole thing. "He is a bad man," Papa said. "I don't care if he is your father. He's bad. He always was and he always will be."

"He used to stop me on the street and ask me about you all and I'd tell him I didn't know much about you," said Nana.

Bad or good, who knew? The answer to that question didn't affect my daily life one way or the other. As 1993 approached, I was nineteen.

And another concern would shortly occupy my life.

A Three-Year Detour, 1990–1993

The days of Tommy the Boxer were about over. He had lost the urge to fight. He didn't have the tiger anymore. He loved getting his protégés, especially John Shea, riled up enough to fight as if the battle was to the death. But he no longer had the rage.

Still, Tommy made a comeback two days before he turned thirty-nine, against a guy thirty-five pounds heavier than he was. He won the decision, four rounds—but that was the last time he got into the ring as a boxer.

Tommy had been practicing with a sparring partner, who was the main belt. The partner had asked Tommy to help him get in shape, and they worked out so hard that Tommy got into boxing shape again, too. "I'll fight, too," he said.

"How about a six-rounder?" the manager asked.

"No way. After five years out o' the ring, no way." He figured that if he was unfairly matched to someone much bigger, he could last four rounds because he could run around and keep the other guy busy enough to outlast him, but wouldn't agree to six rounds.

Tommy described what happened this way:

> So I'm waiting to go in and I hear this music, boom boom boom boom, boom boom boom boom. I see this Mexican or Puerto Rican guy running around the ring with his hat on. He weighed about 170, I weighed 132. I asked, "Who the hell's fighting this guy?"
>
> "You are," they told me. The guy was five divisions

higher than me. They lied about my weight, listing it as 168 pounds. I had on big heavy shoes that made me look a little bigger but they added 35 pounds.

We come out, touch gloves, then the bell rang and I sucker-punched him right off the bat. Both eyes were slit, blood bursting out, and he smiled at me, big grin, and he gave me a wink. I'm thinking, shit, I'm in trouble. I can't hurt him!

So what I did for four rounds was, I boxed the shit out of him. I just tried to wear him out, and I did.

Tommy won, but he quit boxing after that. Whatever animal he once had in him that he had been able to turn on or turn off was gone. He couldn't step into the ring if he wasn't going to try to knock out his opponent. That was the last time he was in a professional ring.

The end of his days as a participant were over, but he had filled his days as a mentor and trainer for several years. He had volunteered under Boston City Parks and Recreation, but the parks had all closed, a state they would remain in for ten or twelve years. Tommy saw the kids running the streets, having nothing to do, and that bothered him. He set up classes to train anyone who wanted to learn how to box at privately-owned gyms like McDonough's. That's how he had first seen Red.

Red's boxing skill was a product of Tommy's guidance, and yet he also learned street smarts from hanging around lower Southie. He developed web-like connections to thugs and crime figures that were part of daily life there. The conventional wisdom in Southie often assumed that a boy or man might get involved in some illegal activities. A gravitation into illegal activity, whether purposeful or by accident, was nothing new or unusual.

I'm an observer, but here's the way I understand Southie. It wasn't the activities themselves that were wrong by definition. The unforgivable wrong was telling the world, especially the cops and feds, about them. The activities themselves were more or less neutral. They were ways for you to make some money to feed yourself and survive. Life was hard. If the opportunity was there in front of you and you had the balls to grab it, you could reap the benefits.

The question I have is this: Did Southie's crime figures take advantage of Red, or did he take advantage of them? The answer might depend on what year you would ask the question. Red's career as assistant to James "Whitey" Bulger started as a test of loyalty in 1985, and he passed it. Since how he got on Bulger's good side is important to what happened to my father four to five years later, I'll summarize what happened, using second-hand information that I can't verify, but am inclined to believe.

Bulger's assistant, Kevin Weeks, who had already had a run-in with Red, called Red to a meeting with Bulger at a local liquor store. Red was taken to the basement and threatened with an Uzi by both Weeks and Bulger. Bulger told Red that Tommy Connors was in trouble and had some heavy debts to Whitey that he hadn't paid off. . . Bulger wanted to know where Tommy hid his money. Red then replied, "Pull the trigger, if you're taking from him . . . then you're taking from me." Finally Bulger uncocked the Uzi and told Red he had passed the test. "You got fucking big balls," he said. "You're loyal. You're one loyal fucking guy. Now you're with me."

The next day twenty-year-old Red became a lieutenant in Bulger's Irish Mob and the boss of Bulger's drug operation. The year was 1985. Tommy knew what was going on, or most of it. Yet he also believed he was a good judge of character and he believed in being loyal to family, and Red was family.

To use one of my father's favorite expressions, "to make a long story short," Tommy insists he did not become a leader in the drug operation Red was running that stretched its long tentacles from South Boston to Florida, though maybe he could have.[8]

Now here's what I think is the truth: he wasn't a leader, but he did make some "visits" to Florida. He hated drug use, but a business opportunity was a business opportunity and he didn't have many ways to make good money. Unknown to Tommy, a bug had been placed on his phone so the DEA could monitor every conversation he had with Red. In all, eventually the feds used sixty-eight phone calls to indict Tommy on conspiracy charges. In one phone call Tommy said something like, "Stick with it like we did before." Tommy denied the conversation meant anything in particular. "I don't know what I meant by that! 'Stick with it?' They said it meant something else." What it meant to the prosecutors was an agreement to continue running cocaine.

At the same time, the authorities were closing in not just on Red Shea, but on a large number of others in the Bulger drug distribution operation. The sting was lengthy. What happened to Shea on August 8, 1990, is now a matter of public record. It can be easily found online and in Shea's book *Rat*

---

[8]The story of what happened to Tommy Connors in this book is one-sided. It's not in any way a decription of the legalities. My purpose is only to summarize my father's version of what happened to him while I was an adolescent in Oklahoma who knew nothing about her father's life. I will let the reader decide if any of Tommy's actions, attitudes, and responses to what life dealth him were or are similar to any of mine.

Bastards, a book in which my father is mentioned often and with admiration.

Shea landed on the front page of the *Boston Herald* the next day. My father was one of fifty-one people rounded up in what the papers described as a sweeping blow to the criminal organization of reputed underworld figure James J. (Whitey) Bulger. The charges ranged from distributing cocaine up to conspiring to operate a criminal narcotics enterprise. Shea was at the top of the list, along with some others: John "Jackie" Mack, 42; Walter Bagley, 38; Thomas "Tommy" Cahill, 42; George "Georgie Boy" Hogan, 44; Tommy Connors, 44; William "Billy" McCarthy, 26; Paul "Pole Cat" Moore, 40; John "Jackie" Cherry, 39; Kevin "Andre the Giant" MacDonald, 33; Edward "Eddie Mac" MacKenzie Jr., 22; Louis "Louie" Sasso, 40; and Jesus Nodarse, 50. Fifty-one at one time. Shea and a few others were charged with running a drug distribution enterprise under the RICO (Racketeer Influenced and Corrupt Organizations) Act.

Shea was sentenced to twenty years. He refused to cooperate with the DEA in "ratting out" other key figures in the operation, and, in fact, he never did, though some of the others arrested eventually did—including, so the story goes, Whitey Bulger himself. We may never know for sure, because Bulger had disappeared. He has been indicted for nineteen murders and remained on the FBI's Ten Most Wanted List until his capture on June 23, 2011. Bulger's picture was right under Osama Bin Laden's on that list.

My father was sentenced to three years on conspiracy charges in federal prison, which he served from 1990 to 1993, two-and-a-half years there and six months in a halfway house with an electronic monitor. His was a relatively light sentence. He believed his arrest was really a way to get to Red, the axle on which the spokes of the Bulger wheel revolved.

In the year 1993 my father was a free man, though one with limited options as an ex-convict. Time for him to avoid the detours and walk the straight and narrow. That was something I was trying to do in Tulsa, but I, too, would take a detour off my one-way path for a short time.

A Detour of My Own, 1991–1994

Wouldn't you think a person would learn from her past? Things were going so well for me. I continued to work for the Still family and I kept my shift at Mazzio's and the chiropractic office. I was trudging through Tulsa Community College but I kept at it. Taking classes that involved writing were very hard and, as with English 101, I had to repeat English 102 twice. Maybe I was slowly improving because I only had to repeat English 201 once.

"Lisa, I want you to get some experience doing office work," Mike told me. "It's a lot easier than having to work in a restaurant the rest of your life." I was happy to work a few hours a week at his office and I learned basic accounting, which has been valuable throughout the years. Mike's colleagues also showed me oil pumps and took me to a couple of fields to see them in action. I soaked up learning like I was dehydrated and finally getting a gulp of water.

Does all work and no play make Jack or Jill dull? I didn't have time to ask that question. Matt, a long-time friend of my brothers, scored tickets to a Steve Miller concert and invited me. I didn't hesitate to accept the offer. My friend Charity upstairs, who I traded off with from time to time, babysat Zackery for me.

Matt was a friend of both of my brothers, a cute guy. He was about three years older than I, and I had known him since I was fourteen. He'd take me places once in a while but our relationship had never been intimate. He seemed to have respect for me.

And then . . . we went to the concert. And we were drinking beers. And we got back to my apartment, and before I had the sense to realize what I was doing, my clothes were off. We were both drunk, and we had sex. One time. It had been close to a year since I had last had sex. But lo and behold, I got pregnant.

Nineteen years old, a mother of a three-year-old, a college student with a full plate, and not just of pizza. I thought I should have an abortion. I was so embarrassed and even angry at myself. I couldn't tell anyone, not even my mom, because I knew I'd hear the whispers: "Again? You mean she didn't learn from the first time? Does she not know about a thing called 'birth control'?" I felt that people would judge me over and over. The old lack of self-confidence and feeling that I was stupid and ugly tried push up out of the back room of my mind again. So stupid, Lisa . . . so stupid. So ignorant. . .

Matt said he'd go with me to an abortion clinic, so I set up an appointment. He offered to pay for half if I'd pay for the other half. I didn't expect what met us outside the building—men, women, and children picketing, holding signs with pictures of aborted fetuses on them and yelling accusations like "baby-killer!"

There in the waiting room sat women of ages that I figured must be anywhere from early teens through my mom's age, maybe older. "I wonder what she's here for," I thought, as I looked around the room at each of them. Some had a companion with them—a mother, a friend, a boyfriend, or even a husband.

A dark-haired boy about Zackery's age kept pulling on his mommy's hand, saying over and over again, "Quiero dulces, Mami!" and pointing outside the door where a vending machine stood. His mother was a girl who looked quite a bit younger than I was. He broke my heart. I looked at Matt out of the corner of my eye. He was leafing through a brochure and didn't seem to notice me or the boy.

"Miss Connor? Come this way."

Matt smiled at me and I handed him my purse. A woman in a smock made of a printed fabric imprinted with puppies and kittens frolicking on it led me into a room that was dimly lit. "First the technician will do an ultrasound," she said. "Go ahead and take off your clothing and jewelry and put it all in the storage locker here. I'll give you a key to it."

She gave me a thin white hospital gown and a young Asian man said to me, "This will feel a little cold at first." He rubbed some jelly that looked like Vaseline on my lower abdomen and moved the camera tool around as he watched a screen. He said nothing. The screen seemed to pulsate a little—something appeared to be moving. Even though I was not supposed to see the screen, my curiosity was up and when he turned his head I sneaked a peek.

"Now, Miss Connor, this is Emily. She'll escort you to the procedure room." A petite nurse led me to a room bare of any decoration or personality. "Doctor will be with you in a moment," she said, smiling. She shuffled a little and she spoke quietly. "You can cover your legs with this," she told me, handling me a plastic-coated paper wrap.

I sat, and sat. And sat. The room was cold. I had taken nothing in with me to read. At first all I could think was, "I wish they'd hurry up, I wish they'd hurry up." But with the passage of the minutes, my thoughts turned to Zackery and how his happy face and wet kisses greeted me when I picked him up after school. I thought of the little boy begging for candy. What disadvantages that child might face not knowing English and with a mother who was a child herself . . . Zackery wouldn't have those disadvantages. . .

Suddenly it became clear to me: I could not do this. I could not go through with it. My fear of being judged for getting pregnant again was the main reason for planning the abortion, and it just wasn't reason enough. I quickly put back on my Levis and t-shirt, left my paper wrap on the table, and opened the locker where I had hung my clothes. I took them into the procedure room and dressed. Before walking back into the waiting room I stopped at the counter and asked for a refund. The workers looked at me, puzzled. They whispered a bit. Maybe they had never had anyone ask for a refund. The compromise was a half refund. I was okay with that.

Matt looked up. "Done already? I expected it to take longer," he said.

"It didn't," I said. "Let's go." I took my purse from him.

As soon as we were outside my confession burst out of me. "I couldn't do it, Matt! I just couldn't! I'm sorry but it's just not for me. I'm a good mom to Zackery and I know I shouldn't have the abortion. I just know."

"Get in the car, Lisa," he said. We climbed in my rattletrap Ford Topaz and he put the keys in the ignition but didn't turn it on. I was afraid to look at him. I'm sure only seconds passed, but it seemed much longer. When he looked at me there were tears in his eyes.

"I'm glad," he said.

We both cried then, hugging each other. "I love you, Lisa," he said. "Let's go shopping for some baby stuff."

So we did. I knew in my heart that I was going to have a girl. We bought lots of pink—blankets, Carter's sleepers, onesies with "I'm my mommy's angel" and other embroidery on them, and, most wonderful, he helped me pick out a new crib. Which I needed—after all, I had thought Zackery would be my only child for a long time and had given the crib to Tim and his wife.

Matt's acceptance of the situation made me feel a little more at ease. Soon after the aborted abortion, he told me he wanted to marry me. I told him I'd think about it.

In the immediate future there were other things I needed to take care of. First, tell Mike, something I dreaded doing. What would he think of me? Would he judge me?

Mike had recently gotten married again. Zackery and I were still staying there when he and his wife needed me.

"Mike, I have something I need to tell you. I hope you won't be too disappointed in me." I just said it simply. "I'm pregnant. I went to have an abortion but I just couldn't do it. I'm going to have the baby."

Here's what Mike Still was, and is, made of: He said, "Lisa, I'm so proud of you for making that decision. Hang on a minute." He went back into his bedroom and then came out with a big wad of bills in his hand. "These are for you, Lisa. You've done so much for my kids and my family. I want you to take this. This is just a bump in the road, and once you get over it you're going to have a beautiful new baby."

I didn't take the money, but could not stop the tears as I hugged him. "Mike, thanks for believing in me, but I'll do this on my own. You know I've always worked hard and I've never had handouts. This is my responsibility, not yours."

He knew me so he didn't argue. "Okay, but if you ever need anything, you know who to ask. I'll always be here for you."

Another vote of confidence and I wasn't sure I deserved it. It was like a good rainfall to an Oklahoma farmer in a drought, though. It kept me plowing on.

Snips, Snails, and Puppy Dog's Tails, May 30, 1994

Matt and I did not get married, but he started staying at my apartment. After some time went by I asked how much money he made. His response was, "That's none of your business." An argument brewed and soon into it he grabbed hold of me and shoved me up against the wall. His forcefulness combined with the look in his eyes frightened me.

"Leave! Now!" I demanded. He argued, but he did. I told myself, "Lisa, be focused, be strong." So I kept working, nannying, and going to school as usual. Occasionally I had men hit on me. It's funny, though, or maybe not––as my stomach swelled bigger and bigger, the men showed less and less interest. I know it's said that there is nothing prettier than a pregnant woman, but from what I can tell, it's usually fathers-to-be who say it. Other men didn't act as if they thought so. The men who had previously flirted with me began to have a hands-offish attitude toward me. No one, not my fellow employees or my customers, teased me, though. I think I had a "don't mess with me" attitude. (Tommy's daughter? Maybe.)

Mike helped me find a larger and nicer place to live, a duplex. One of the biggest blessings in it was a washer and dryer hook up. I had plenty of money saved to purchase one, but I shopped for a couple of weeks looking for the absolute best price I could find.

Like my mom and Guy had done when I was a kid, I made the dining room into a bedroom. That way I could have a room for Zackery and a room for the little girl who'd be there before long. This duplex was bigger and nicer than the one I grew up in.

Zackery and I spent time with my best friend, Sherry, and her family.

Sherry had grown up in foster care but had found a nice family when she was a teenager. We talked a lot about our families. She still had contact with her siblings and sometimes her biological mother. Her sister came to live with her for a short time. We all had to be careful around her sister, especially if any of us had any open wounds or cuts, because she found out she had hepatitis. Sherry told me about a phone call her sister had been dreading as she awaited some test results. Her sister wouldn't tell Sherry what the call was about. We imagined, though what the news might be, we weren't sure until Sherry actually found out the news. I loved encouraging Sherry to always strive to be the best person she could be regardless of how difficult her family situation was.

Mom and Dempsey came over occasionally, but for the most part I was on my own and I liked it that way. I was about done at Tulsa Community College. My grades weren't honor society level, but they had improved slowly. I was thinking of where I would go next. There was not even the faintest doubt in my mind that I would continue my education. I had worked too hard to give up.

First, though, was what lay more immediately ahead. Matt started coming around again a month or so before I was due to go into labor. He promised to go with me to the hospital. Memorial Day, May 30, 1994, the little baby whose life started as a result of an evening hearing a live performance of "Fly Like an Eagle" was born. As I lay on the table in the delivery room, head propped up with a couple pillows, legs spread apart, we heard his cry: Trey Matthew Connors, weighing in at almost ten pounds. What a beautiful—and big—surprise.

Matt moved in. He made it very clear that he didn't want me to know how much money he made, saying he didn't think it was any of my business. A warning bell? Maybe, but if it rang, my ears didn't pick up the sound.

Matt presented me with an engagement ring and shortly after the birth I went to work at a nearby restaurant where I could work for tips. The tips were good, very good.

Matt would watch both the boys when his work schedule didn't conflict with mine. But something began to happen, not overnight, but over a period of several months. When I'd get home from work he'd question me. "So . . . were you a good girl tonight? Did anyone try to hit on you?" He'd remark, "I don't like the idea of men leering at you and staring at your butt!"

He didn't have anything to worry about, but I think he'd already made up his mind that I was flirting at work. He kept talking about how hard my job was and how he wished I didn't have to be on my feet slinging drinks and carrying hot trays. I didn't guess at the purpose behind a suggestion he made. "Lisa, my mom has a house in Wagoner," he told me. "We can get really cheap rent there and it's nice."

I reluctantly said, "Okay." It would mean I wouldn't be working for the first time since I'd had children, but I could go to Northeastern State University in Tahlequah, which was about twenty miles from Wagoner. We moved to Wagoner with Matt. We could be the family I had never had. But it wasn't long before I began to wonder if I had made a mistake.

I soon suspected that the reason for the move was not to save money but so he could have control. He wanted to know about everywhere I went. I didn't appreciate having to report about every detail of my school schedule. In fact, I don't think he wanted me to go to school at all. I was used to taking care of myself, and I resented having to check in. I felt more and more restricted, watched, not trusted. Our relationship deteriorated over the course of six months or so. Without a foundation of mutual trust and respect to ground our relationship, jealousy and resentment eroded it.

The breaking point came after a nice evening with Matt's family. Grandma Linda and Granny, Matt's mother and grandmother, came for an afternoon and dinner. They taught me some simple recipes I had never cooked before. We had a nice visit that evening, but Matt had been drinking beer, and after they left, trouble started. I honestly don't know what triggered argument, but next thing I knew he grabbed me and pushed me so hard that I nearly went through the window.

I was pretty scared, but more so, I was worried about the boys. I tried to take the boys and leave but he wouldn't let me out the door with my precious boys. He blocked the door and looked so menacing that I backed off. "You're not going anywhere, Lisa. Not with those two boys!"

I had no choice but to stay, but I made the condition very clear. "If you ever touch me again, I will leave you."

Matt just looked at me. Trey was sleeping in his crib but Zackery had begun to cry a little. I went into his room to comfort him. I turned the light back on and read to him, and I said, "I love you always and forever. Pointing to him and then to me, I started again, "We love each other—"

Zackery helped me finish the sentence: "—Always and forever."

All quiet on the Matt-and-Lisa front for a short time. Then it collapsed like a house built on stilts in a hurricane when Trey, still a baby, came down with Respiratory Syncytial Virus (RSV), that dangerous respiratory infection that affects mostly children.

I had him in and out of the doctor's. With the first symptoms, I took him to the doctor and started trying to follow instructions on treating him at home. I set the alarm for every hour to suction out his nose. I elevated his crib and we put a breathing machine in his room. I tried to get him admitted to the hospital, but the doctors just kept saying, "Bring him back, bring him back."

I didn't know what RSV was until Mom told me she had seen some cases admitted to pediatrics at Tulsa's St. John's Hospital where she still worked. She had seen babies who were very ill and a few who had even passed away. I didn't know for sure if RSV was what Trey had, but I was very scared because he had all the symptoms.

It was a stressful time for all four of us. I continued to get up every hour to tend to Trey. "Let him sleep. He'll be okay," Matt would mumble sleepily as I jumped out of bed for the fifth time one night. He did not make an offer to help—whether he thought it was my job or just that he didn't think Trey was all that sick, I didn't know. He'd just glare at me the next morning as he poured himself a cup of coffee. I could see the resentment on his face. And I was tired, very tired. I needed help I didn't feel I was getting.

Another evening just after I finished suctioning Trey's nose again and had lay him in his crib, Matt arrived home from work and found me on the phone with Sherry. He jumped on top of me, broke the telephone, and started strangling me.

"Ma . . . a . . . at . . . get off me!" Wheezing, I tried to fight him but he was too strong. I tried gasping for air. I couldn't breathe. I tried to pry his hands off my neck. I was losing strength, and I thought, "This is it. I am going to die." I started to fade into in an unconscious state. I was scared, more than I had ever been scared before, and I was helpless.

Finally, he let go and got off of me. I cried. I got up, went into Trey's bedroom, and sat down on the floor watching him struggle to breathe as he slept. He's not going to let me leave, especially with the boys. I don't know what was worse—the terror or the hopelessness.

So I didn't. I didn't do anything. I didn't think Zackery saw what happened but I suspected he heard it. The look on his small face later told me he knew it had happened. I tucked him in bed and we read and went through our nighttime ritual of saying we loved each other "always and forever."

Later that same night Trey's condition deteriorated. "I'm taking Trey to ER," I announced. I put Zackery in the car along with Trey and we drove to the hospital. I did not ask Matt his opinion—we just went. They admitted Trey and he was in for three or four days. Sherry took Zackery during the time Trey was in the hospital.

Once again, in a medical setting I had time to do nothing but think. I sat by Trey's bed and asked myself if the relationship with Matt had any future. Should we get married? That seemed a terrible idea, though he was pushing for it. Should I just make the best of the situation and go on in the status quo? I did not want someone controlling me, and the more I balked at it, the more controlling Matt became. I did not want my children to be raised in an abusive home.

My OB/GYN must have heard we were in the hospital. He came to the room to see Trey and me. I had put on a turtleneck hoping to hide the bruises from Matt's attempt to strangle me, but I guess the doctor noticed something, because he walked over and pulled the top edge of my turtleneck down a little. Then he said, "Ms. Connor, something has happened. I want you to go down to the ER right now and have them take pictures of your bruises. What is it that happened?" he asked.

"Nothing, don't worry about me." I couldn't tell the truth. I don't know why I was so afraid of telling him what had happened.

The doctor eventually assessed Trey's condition as good enough for me to take him home after five overnights in the hospital. Matt was already at work when we got back to the house in Wagoner. I had come up with a plan, so I spent that day before he got home packing boxes and storing them behind the garage where he would not be likely to look on a weeknight.

We barely spoke to each other that evening, but that was not unusual. The next day I did the same thing. Again, a sullen evening. It would be our last together, though he didn't seem to suspect anything. I planned to do exactly what I told Matt I would do if he ever touched me again.

As soon as he left for work I had a friend get the U-Haul truck I had reserved and bring it to the house. Several guys she knew came over and in less than a couple hours they had everything I wanted to take with the boys and me loaded up securely.

So Matt and I were no longer a couple—but that didn't mean Matt was out of my life. He was Trey's father and I knew I'd see him soon. We stayed with my mom for a week. I had given her money awhile back to hold in a savings account just in case I ever had an emergency. Did I know this was going to happen? I don't think so—it was just "me" to have money tucked away.

Still, this was money he didn't know about. I took that money and paid a deposit on an apartment. Time to get off the detour and get back on the highway to an education. As far as NSU, well, I just stopped going to classes when Trey became so sick and I never even officially withdrew.

I had taken Zackery back to the day care center in Tulsa that he had gone to previously but it wouldn't take Trey because he was too young. The solution? I got a job at a day care center where I could take Trey with me. It allowed me to keep tabs on him. I thought it was a good place, but like everyone else, I had heard the stories about day care center abuse. This way I didn't have to hope Trey was being treated well—I could see for myself. And when Trey was almost old enough, Zackery's center took him a little earlier than they usually would have. I was so thankful they made this concession for us.

Because I had to work and believed in work, Lone Star Steakhouse in Tulsa became my next employer. I knew both Zackery and Trey were in an excellent day care center and I worked the lunch shift throughout the weekdays. My tips were very good, and I worked there taking the late shift, meaning I stayed on the floor until the next shift arrived, and then later worked on weekends. I worked there for four years. As with Mazzio's, I also developed a group of regular customers, which made my income fairly predictable.

Here's a key to success as a waitress: be pleasant and be efficient. Act like you like the people you're serving. You'll get repeat business. That wasn't hard for me. I was discovering, in fact had already discovered, that talking to people, both adults and children, was natural for me.

I also cleaned houses. I'd get up Saturday morning, load the boys into the Topaz, take them with me or to a friend's, and clean a house.

Some Tulsa trivia: One of the houses I cleaned belonged to the mother of the comedian Sam Kinison, a Tulsa boy. He had already been killed in a car accident near Needles, California when I started working for her. Sam had been quite the character. He had a big presence, often wearing long dark trench coats and spouting vitriolic humor. His routines were edgy with lots of references to drugs, but his trademark scream is what he'll probably always be remembered for. He became famous, incorporating the song "Wild thing, wild thing, you make my heart sing" into his act. He's buried in Tulsa, and I think his mother still lives in the same house that I cleaned.

And so, alone again, I was at peace with my decision to break off my relationship with Matt. What I didn't know was that Matt had a private investigator follow me, and that while I was happily pulling the kids in the wagon, swimming with them, doing all the things mothers and their children do. I was being watched.

Back and Forth and Back and Forth, 1995–1998

It never occurred to me that it might be hard to convince a university to let me in—my grades were barely adequate. I had not even turned twenty-two. I was about the same age as some of the pretty, carefree-looking senior girls and tanned boys in shorts and flip-flops that threw Frisbees to each other on the green, but they didn't even give me a second glance as I wheeled a baby in a stroller and held a four-year-old boy's sweaty little hand in mine. I carried a rejection letter I had already received from my application to attend Oklahoma State University (OSU) and a transcript from Tulsa CC in my purse and I went from office to office to office at Oklahoma State University. I didn't know who to ask to admit me for the fall 1995 semester. I got turned down or sent elsewhere at least a dozen times. I didn't even understand the hierarchy of administration. All I knew is that I was in the administration building, and I deserved a chance. I certainly wasn't going to accept "No" as an answer. I didn't have to. Finally, I heard the words: "Someone give her a chance." The offer was a probationary one, but I was in. No more "slippin', slippin', slippin' into the future." The future had arrived. I would be a student again the upcoming fall semester, 1995.

I prepared to move to Stillwater, not knowing that there might be another roadblock in my way. "There's no one like a woman scorned." So goes the saying most of us have heard. I'm going to rewrite it: "There's no force in nature like a man scorned." I had hurt Matt's feelings, big time. He was going to make me pay. I don't blame him. We were not a good match, but when a relationship goes sour, there is usually blame to be shared by both.

Matt took me to court. He tried to get custody not just of Trey but also of Zackery. He hired the most powerful attorney in Tulsa. He moved in with his father, and was able to use all of his money to hire an attorney. I didn't know what to do—all I knew was that I had to get an attorney, too.

When we moved to Stillwater for me to go to school, I had to drive back and forth to Tulsa for court dates. By this time, I had learned about student loans and knew I was eligible. My student loan money went for something I imagine most students don't use it for—a good attorney. Nana also sent me some money, a sizeable chunk. I didn't ask her for it. She just wanted to help.

I'm not sure why Matt was so determined to get custody not only of Trey but also of Zackery. Trey, yes, but why Zackery? His attorney's approach was to try to prove I was an unfit mother. But he couldn't, because I was a very good mother. There was nothing to use against me. Eventually we got the custody issues sorted out and he got visitation rights for Trey. I found out later that he had private investigators follow me and put phone taps in my car.

But for a while the case dragged on and on. That first semester in Stillwater, I don't think I made even a C average. I was back and forth to Tulsa, back and forth to Tulsa for court dates, and I was also trying to work as many hours as I could handle. Child care was always a challenge, but I kept telling myself, you do what you have to do. I became friends with my neighbors and their son or daughter would babysit on occasion. Still, they couldn't watch Trey and Zackery all the time, because they had lives, too.

Because I had to work and believed in work . . . I continued working at Lone Star Steakhouse in Tulsa on weekends. I put a lot of mileage on my ancient Topaz, and the boys spent a lot of time in the car. Does it seem odd that I'd live in Stillwater and drive seventy miles to work in Tulsa? I needed the tips, and college students in Stillwater were notoriously bad tippers.

We'd drive to Tulsa, where I'd work a double shift at Lone Star. I'd pick up extra shifts because someone always needed time off—lots of college students working there. If and when I needed money and when my schedule would allow, I would call the management at Lone Star Steakhouse and ask if I could come in. Employee turnover in most restaurants is pretty high so they always appreciated having a dependable worker on the schedule. Plus, I often increased sales with my customers and helped them feel good about it, too. Eventually, I developed a regular showing of customers and often the restaurant would get calls asking if I was working on particular weekends. Whew. It makes me tired just to write about those days. Most weekends I worked about thirty hours in addition to trying to keep up on my class assignments.

Those weekends I was in Tulsa I usually asked Matt's mother, "Grandma Linda," and his grandmother, "Granny," to watch the boys while I was at work, and they seemed happy to do that. By "work," I really mean *work:* I was on the floor until closing time on Friday nights, then usually I talked someone else at the restaurant into giving me a shift so I would do a double shift on Saturdays, then the lunch shift on Sundays.

And I started going to church, a first for me. When the boys and I were in Stillwater we went to a little Methodist church near the house where we lived. When I was in Tulsa we went to a Baptist church before I'd work a Sunday afternoon shift. The church people were very pleasant and some of them would come in so I could wait on them at Lone Star.

I loved waiting on them. An extrovert was emerging. Watered by praise from my customers and management, my personality had begun flowering at Mazzio's and it was in bloom, though I don't know I would have labeled myself as an extrovert at the time. All I knew was that I got energized by being with people, and they seemed to like to be around me. My mom said, "I don't know where you came from! You sure didn't get your personality from me!" She'd smile, but I think she knew. I didn't, though. I had no idea that in many ways I was a taller, blonder version of an ex-convict who lived nearly two thousand miles away from Tulsa.

Scotty and the Venita Years, 1996–2002

"Little sister, you can do it," Scotty used to often say to me when I was a teenager. Scotty was a very energetic guy, maybe even hyperactive. He was a dare-devil. People often compare my personality to my father's but I think Scotty may have been even more like him. He had the Irish looks, too, and relatively short height, no taller than I was.

In contrast, Tim was tall and looked more like the Lithuanian side of the family. He was more laid-back, with a low-key personality like my mother's, or at least, that was how I would have described him then. He was quiet and didn't reveal much of what he really thought about anything. He got good grades and all of us characterized him as "the smart one"— and, as is probably already apparent, they characterized me as "the slow one," a self-image that took me years to overcome.

Since Tim was six years older than me and probably because we had such different personalities, we weren't very close. When I remember him as a teenager, something occurs to me that might reveal his feelings about living in Tulsa and about our stepfather, Guy, who would have still been with my mother when Tim graduated from high school: Tim was off to Oklahoma State University almost immediately. He never came home to live after that; in fact, he rarely came home even to visit.

Though very different personalities, Tim and Scott were still close as kids and they had some mutual friends. As an adolescent, Scotty teamed with Tim and together they didn't have much use for me, as they say in the South. When Tim went to college my relationship with Scott became closer than it had been when Tim was around. I guess we drew together, two teenage siblings with a mom who was either working or sleeping most of the time we were awake. Scotty had graduated from high school, barely, and was planning to go into a technical college nearby to study robotics. He continually encouraged me to get my high school diploma and he made me feel as if I just might have what it took to make it.

Of the three of us, Scotty was the one who asked Mom the most questions about our dad. Then he'd tell me how Mom had answered, which was always in an unsatisfying way, as if we were on a "need-to-know" basis and didn't need to know much.

Scotty enrolled in the robotics program after graduating high school, but he failed out of it. Then he disappeared for a while. By the time Scotty came home, I was a sixteen-year-old mom. Sometimes Scotty's pep talks were the main thing that kept me going. I tried to encourage him, too. I wished he'd smile more, though I knew why he didn't. Crooked teeth are so easy to correct! And they can do so much damage to a person's self-image. I began to see they had virtually molded Scotty's personality, and yet I had no way to fix that.

While we got along well, our relationship wasn't enough to keep Scotty home. It got to where he'd disappear for days at a time. Eventually he'd resurface, and it would be obvious he had been doing drugs of some kind or another. I would smell the pot on his clothing. He didn't even try to hide that habit much.

Then unexpectedly came one of those events that ended up shaping his life. "Are you Scott's mother?" The policeman stood on the other side of the screen rocking on his toes. His sunglasses were mirrored and I could see myself in them as I stood there holding Zackery.

"Why? I asked.

"We have picked up your son and we need you to come down to the precinct. He's in a heap o' trouble."

"Hold on a minute, I'll go get Mom," I said. I tiptoed into her bedroom and shook her shoulder. "Mom . . . Mom!" She opened her eyes.

"What's the matter, Lisa?" she mumbled, her eyes still closed.

"Mom, a policeman is here and he says Scotty has been arrested!"

She sat up quickly. "What is it this time?" she muttered, more to herself than to me. Her feet hit the floor and she quickly threw on some capris and a t-shirt.

We had not heard from my brother for several weeks but that was not unusual. Turned out this time he had gotten into some mischief. He had used a Magic Marker to write "Scott Connor" on a brick, and then, maybe on a dare, who knows—he had tossed it through a nearby restaurant window.

If that were all, he might have just gotten a slap on the wrist and have been sent home. But a restaurant customer claimed he had seen a gun in Scott's hand. That meant an attorney, which my mother certainly could not afford. Since having a gun was a felony, it also meant Scotty would be in jail until the case could be sorted out.

A detective got a search warrant and next thing we knew the little room where Scotty had been staying in a friend's house was being turned upside down to find a gun that I am sure to this day was not ever there. The police found nothing incriminating, no drugs as far as I know, which was a small miracle because I knew Scotty was using, and not just marijuana.

I am not exactly sure what happened to Scotty during that time in jail, but he must have had a psychotic meltdown. What I saw was Scotty's behavior, which I think was partly an outcome of what had happened, not the explanation for it. Maybe he became incoherent or obnoxious. Maybe it's where the delusional behavior that we observed later in him began. Neither Mom nor I knew exactly why he ended up being moved and we had no good lawyer who could find out for us. Whatever the reason, the authorities had him moved to a state psychiatric facility that had a lock-up unit, and he was not released from that floor for two years. I wonder now if things would have turned out the way they did if we had had good legal representation.

It was a slow downhill slide for Scotty from that point. The facility was awful. Very bad. It was in Venita and was state-run and run down. The staff mixed Scotty right in with the worst of psychotics, such as a man who had decapitated somebody. Scotty was afraid there, especially at night. There was little pretense made of really helping these people. The care was mainly what they called "custodial"—what you might more accurately call "warehousing." I had both the boys by the time the Tulsa jail put him there. Though the distance was 180 miles from Stillwater to Venita, I would drive to see him, sometimes loading Zackery and Trey in the car. Visits from the boys and me usually cheered him up.

After an unusually busy semester that kept me from seeing him for three months or so, one school holiday I took the boys to Venita to see him. The orderly led him out to the lobby to meet us. "Hi, boys," he said. "Come sit on my knee."

They looked at me and I'm afraid I was still in a state of confusion as to who I was looking at, so I nodded a little uncertainly. There sat an overweight man with dark, unkempt, longish hair and a beard that was still coming in. I had never seen him look like that before.

"Children, do not be afraid of me," he said. He patted them on their heads. And my thoughts came together: Scotty was acting like Jesus.

Oh . . . my . . . God. Zackery and Trey were antsy, as boys are. I don't think they were afraid of Scott, and I can't say I was exactly afraid of him, either. But I was at a loss for understanding what was going on. He proceeded to quote Bible verses, or what sounded like Bible verses to me. Our conversation was so strange.

After we got back to Stillwater, I called Mom to tell her about Scotty's unusual behavior. She saw it for herself the next time Dempsey drove her to Venita. Mom was afraid to drive on the highway so she always had to coordinate her trips with either Dempsey, a friend, or me taking her. She was lost as to what was going on in Scott's brain. He was on a huge number of medications, some of them not out long enough to know long-term side effects. One of the nurses told me the staff psychiatrist was trying to get what she termed Scotty's "schizophrenia" under control, but he hadn't yet found quite the right dosage.

I visited him pretty regularly. I always took him something to eat, which he devoured right in front of the boys and me. We had tried the cafeteria food once and I knew full well why he seemed so famished. I would have been, too, if I had had to eat it. It was bland and soft, with lots of mashed things for people who had few teeth, and it was starch-heavy. Maybe that's why he seemed to have gained more weight each time I saw him.

Eventually his behavior began to be more like the Scotty we knew. He talked less about how he was Jesus reincarnated, and the staff psychiatrist judged him well enough to receive a day pass. I would check him out for the day and we'd go to lunch or a movie or both and then to the local Braum's ice cream shop.

In spite of Scott's fragile mental state, he always perked up when he asked me what was happening in my life. "Wow, little sister, you are doing great," he'd say.   When his behavior and mentality seemed to be stabilizing, Mom and Dempsey would go get him and bring him back to their house for the weekend or a couple days at a time. He was really improving, or so it seemed much of the time.

But then there would be incidents that would frighten all of us, and we didn't know how to sort them out. On one weekend visit, I remember Mom, Scotty, and I in the car going somewhere. I was sitting in the back seat, Mom was driving, and Scotty was sitting next to her.

Without warning he went into a panic state. He began to talk what I can only describe as crazy talk. "Mom, they're in my brain! Mom, they're after us, they're gonna get us!"

What should a person do in such a situation? I probably would have done something different from what my mom did. She merely said in an exasperated tone, "Scotty, you know that isn't true. Now shut up unless you can talk about something else."

So he did—and maybe that was the right response to his rant that day.

Scott's diagnosis was "paranoid schizophrenia." A couple more years went by. He seemed to be improving, though he would call me or my mom sometimes three, four times a day or more. Nana called me several times to tell me Scotty had written her a card or had sent her a long letter.

Eventually he was free to come out of the lock-up facility in Venita and was placed in a group home there on the grounds. The atmosphere was an improvement even aside from the facilities themselves. It meant he could be with people with conditions similar to his, people who were trying to live a semblance of a normal life under some minimal supervision. No more psychopaths and severe cases as his daily companions. Eventually he moved out of the central group home and into a three bedroom pre-fab home on the grounds. There was a nurse's station and other houses within walking distance. Things seemed to be looking up for him, and we were all cautiously relieved.

There was one nagging concern, though: Scotty's weight. The lack of physical activity, experimental medications, and too much cheap food may have been, in effect, the catalysts for some lingering physical issues that should not have been problems for a man his age.

A Not-So-Still Life in Stillwater, 1994–1997

"Lisa, we have something for you." I was on first-name acquaintance basis with the young guy, Paul, who ran the register at the QuikTrip. I said "Hi" to Maria and Wilson, two "members" of the unofficial coffee club who were nearly always sipping a quick cup when I pulled in before school or work to fill my old Topaz with gas. It was showing its age. Every other week it would break down. One morning it wouldn't start after filling the gas tank, so one of the coffee lovers grabbed a screwdriver out of his car and got it going again by sticking it in the choke. It had gotten to be a regular thing for me to run into the store to borrow a screwdriver.

Paul was standing with his arms behind his back. "Here ya go, I think you can use this more than we can." He handed me a long screwdriver as Maria and Wilson clapped.

"It's our gift to you, Lisa," Maria said. "Enjoy it in good health. Salud!" She took a sip of her latte.

"And you know what to do with it!" Wilson smiled.

OSU was overwhelming at first and not just because my car was so temperamental. During my first semester, I often had to run to one court appearance or consultation after another and I barely passed my classes. Once the custody issues were resolved about a year later, I did better, but I discovered I would often have to study all night. Research papers were the toughest challenge for me. I had had such a poor education. I had never learned how to do them, and I wasn't sure where to start. Over and over and over again I would write and write and write. "Never give in. Never give in," I repeated to myself. I often took my boys to the library with me, especially the first year after moving to Stillwater. If you are the mother of boys, you know what I mean when I say those study evenings were, um, interesting. Those study carrels were perfect places to hide under and not be seen, and those "stacks," as the library calls them, row after narrow row, were seemingly made for the actual purpose of playing hide 'n' seek or tag. I tried to keep Zackery and Trey quiet, but I got so preoccupied copying down facts and figures or feeding dimes into the copy machine that I did sometimes temporarily lose track of them.

A story about one evening at Edmon Low Library will show how single-minded I was when it came to getting my studies done. I was sitting at one of the big Formica-topped study tables, books about the Vietnam War spread out all around me, trying to fill in 4" x 6" note cards with quotations for a history term paper. I guess I was so used to the loud whispers and chatter of two young boys that I just tuned Zackery and Trey out. I didn't notice that they were having an even greater, and a bit louder, time than usual.

A group of five or six students was sitting near me. They would whisper or talk softly to each other from time to time, but I paid little attention to them.

"Excuse me, ma'am. If you can't keep your boys quiet we'd like to request that you leave the library." Since it didn't register at first that the girl was talking to me, she got up from her seat and came over to get my attention. "Ma'am. Ma'am!"

I looked up at a pretty brunette girl standing over me. "Excuse me?" I said.

"Ma'am, we're trying to study here and your children are bothering us."

My reaction was immediate. Five feet, nine inches of pent-up emotion, I got up and stood over the little group. "Well . . . let me explain something to you." By that time everyone at the table had raised their heads and all were listening to me. "I deserve an education as much as you do. I'm paying for it, and I am going to get it. I have no one to watch my two boys. I need to be in the library." I paused a minute and looked at the group. A couple of them looked away a little. Two boys were snickering. The pretty girl merely looked at me with no expression on her face. "Do I have a volunteer to babysit for me? I can't find a babysitter. Do I have a volunteer?"

Nothing, no response. I waited a minute. I walked back to my table. "I'll tell the boys to quiet down, but no, I am not leaving. If you don't like it, there are plenty of tables in other areas."

It's probably a "duh" statement to say my Stillwater days were hard ones. Finances were—duh again—tight even though I always made sure I had a savings. Mike Still continued to help me in little roundabout ways, never stepping out of bounds. His father lived in Stillwater and he came to visit him from time to time. One afternoon Mike showed up at the front door when I was trying to write a paper on my typewriter I had purchased at a nearby pawn phop. I was, as usual, overwhelmed. He checked in my cupboard to make sure we had food and said, "Lisa, if there's anything I can do, I want to help. So does Theresa" (his wife by this time). Mike knew that I had a lot of pride and wouldn't ask for help. Once he showed up with a computer that he claimed he didn't need any more. So finally I had my own computer to work on at home while the boys were sleeping.

When he dropped by one day he told me about his father and how lonely he was. It was the one-year anniversary of the day his wife, Mike's mother, had passed away, and Mike's brothers and sister didn't check on him much. Mike said his dad wasn't eating well and he was worried about him.

I asked, "Where does your father live?" Mike had done so much for me and I thought the least I could do was help him by looking after his elderly father. A few days after that conversation I thought, I'm just going to stop by and see how he's doing. I pulled in the driveway and rang his bell.

"Hi, Grandpa Lee, I'm Lisa," I said.

"I know who you are, Lisa. Mike has told me about how you're going to OSU," he said. "Come on in."

As soon as I walked in the living room I could not only see but also smell the dust and mustiness. I told him I'd sweep and dust a little and I looked in his cupboard. The only thing on the shelf besides some stale Oreo cookies and potato chips was Dinty Moore Beef Stew—ugh.

A couple days later I made some fried chicken and mashed potatoes for Zackery, Trey, and me. I'll just run these leftovers to Grandpa Lee, I thought. From that point on, whenever I cooked more than just frozen pizza I loaded the boys in the Topaz and took a meal over to him and we had a nice time eating together.

He swiftly became Grandpa Lee to my boys. There was a tire swing in his back yard and he seemed to enjoy pushing the boys as high as he could on it. Watching them, I thought about how good it was for my sons to be around a male role model, sort of a grandfather to them. At any rate, Zackery and Trey had the willing attention of Grandpa Lee meanwhile. He became the grandfather that the boys did not have on either side of their biological family.

And Grandpa Lee did some very nice things for me, not to mention trying to match me up to any young man he thought might make a good catch. He had my car towed to a service station more than once. We'd go there together and he'd say, "Now, Lisa, that young mechanic has a crush on you. I bet he has a nice big home and would be very nice to you." It really got funny when he tried to hook me up with another son of his.

"Lisa, my son is very wealthy, very successful. Wouldn't you like to meet him?"

"Now, Grandpa Lee, isn't he like forty years old?"

We both laughed. But I thought his concern for me was sweet. Every so often he would insist on giving me some money and I would say "no." But when I buckled the boys into the Topaz there would be some dollar bills stuck under my windshield wiper. Grandpa Lee would always deny he knew where they came from. Like father, like son. It made me feel good to help Grandpa Lee whether it was bringing him food or cleaning his house. I felt like it was just a small way I could repay Mike for everything he had done for me over the years. Just knowing how much Mike cared for my boys helped me feel better about myself.

I made the most out of my weekdays while the boys were in school or daycare, making every minute of my time count. I continued going to classes and alternating between cleaning houses and working for the non-profits. On weekdays I had most late afternoons and evenings free to spend time with the boys before their bed time. We dined at restaurants some, where I

taught them manners and the importance of thanking all levels of workers–
–that was something very important to me, having worked for so long as a
server. We went for walks to the local park or we went to movies. Zack was
eventually old enough to go to school in Stillwater. He got involved in summer T-ball and then in coach-pitched baseball, and he joined Cub Scouts,
too.

Bedtime was a very special, very close, time for the boys and me. There
is something indescribable about the sweetness of a little boy just out of the
tub or shower, hair still wet, teeth brushed, eyes sparkling, smelling like
Johnsons & Johnsons baby soap, that I loved. Each night, we read books together and talked about our day. Then I tucked my precious boys into their
beds, kissed them, and said "I love you."

Next item on the day's agenda was my "nightlife." Out would come
the dust cloth and mop. Polish, sweep, swab, empty trash. My solitary nighttime cleaning chores finished, my own private study hall would begin. I'd
often be buried in books and papers all night and when I say "all night," I
literally mean all night. I estimate that due to my lack of previous good education, it probably took me five times as long to write a paper or complete
a homework assignment as it took the average student.

And so went the not-so-still Stillwater days, in a busy but comfortable
routine. I was accumulating credits. I had taken a couple of classes that I felt
drawn to in Family and Community Studies, and had chosen my major of
Family Relations and Child Development, with a cognate of Individual,
Family and Community Services. In 1997, I met a man on campus who
would become very important to me and the boys, and, at about the same

time, I did an internship in my major that would help me see the direction my career would take.

AN END AND A BEGINNING, 1996–1998

Without the boys in tow, I probably looked like a typical college student on the Stillwater campus. I dressed like them in shorts or Levi's, and many of the girls, particularly the sorority girls it seemed, had long blonde hair like mine. I was certainly in the same age bracket as many of the students. Yet I'm pretty sure there was not another upper division student my age who was already the mother of two young boys or who had to fight in court over their custody, nor one who took advantage of every break between classes to clean someone else's house.

I was atypical in so many ways, but as I became inevitably more involved in my classes, I became in some ways a typical college student. I finally gained a little savvy about how to navigate the maze of options for financial help so I could graduate. I was approved for a work-study program and I started it at Lincoln Alternative Academy in summer 1997, the beginning of my junior year. What a great fit for a graduate of an alternative school to work in an alternative school, I thought.

Lincoln Alternative Academy is one of the Stillwater Public Schools. To understand how it operated when I was there, you'd have to read between the lines: "The mission of the Lincoln Alternative Academy staff is to provide quality individualized instruction and personal support. We will strive to instill a commitment to the development of self-worth, life skills training and academic preparation that allows both students and staff the opportunity to reach their full potential in life." The quality of the education was some big steps up the ladder from what I had received in Tulsa. I loved the kids. I especially enjoyed the extracurricular activities with the students. We played basketball, volleyball, flag football, so many of the sports I loved. I liked the atmosphere there and the staff made me feel valued and appreciated, a feeling which I always ate up like I was starving. I was offered a job there on the part-time staff. As I worked with the students on their schoolwork, I realized I was learning a lot of the material alongside them. I kept that secret to myself, though. I absorbed the information like a sponge. When I had to leave for a 1997 summer internship program, one of the counselors wrote an evaluation of my work. Here's what it said:

"She contributed positively to our workplace. . . .I was very pleased with Lisa's willingness and ability to help staff and students with a variety of tasks. Lisa showed initiative by seeking out things to do rather than waiting to be told. I found Lisa to be adaptable and flexible to change . . . she enthusiastically took on new responsibilities and saw them through. . . .The quality of her work was exceptional. Lisa was well liked by the students and staff . . . because of her smiling personality and willingness to work alongside us."

Pretty high praise, and I knew it. He went on to recommend me to the Payne County Youth Services, where I could complete the internship that was a requirement for my Bachelor of Science degree program.

My year at Lincoln Alternative was my first venture into a job that was somewhat related to the degree program I was finishing. I stayed there a year. When I had time off, the boys and I still visited and ate as often as we could with Grandpa Lee and some weekends I continued working at Lone Star Steakhouse in Tulsa. Grandpa Lee began to tell me more and more about his children and his beloved wife. They sounded like what I thought of as a typical American family, different from my own in so many ways. Yet the family had grown apart over the years. Without the wife and mother as the anchor, the family had gone adrift a little. There were four children. The brothers still were close, but the daughter had separated herself emotionally from the rest of them and, as an extended family, they didn't get together much.

At the least, Grandpa Lee told me, he'd like to be closer to his grandchildren. Hmmm. I knew an easy way to make that happen. I had slumber parties for the cousins at his house. I took charge of them so he didn't have to do much but be there and enjoy the fun. Mike brought Andrew and Leah from Tulsa, and I also invited the Stillwater cousins.

The kids had such a good time together that I decided to expand the gatherings to include the parents. Why not? I thought. I didn't really expect all of them to come, but they did. In summer of 1996, we had a big cookout for the Still family at Grandpa Lee's house and every sibling came. They had a very nice time visiting together and some family strings were retied.

I didn't realize this until much later, but I owe something to Mike Still's family that I doubt has ever occurred to them. They don't realize it, but that barbecue might rank as one of the first planned events of "Lisa, the Professional Event Planner." My business dreams had not yet coalesced, but I can look back at early instances such as that one and see where my talents and my personality were taking me.

But I'm going to back up just a little because a couple of other events, both of them firsts, changed my life in that same year at OSU: First, I went on a cruise, the first totally fun trip I had ever taken. That experience indirectly led to the second event.

I became "Lisa Ditchkoff, Married Lady." No, the end of my days as a not-so-carefree single mother did not happen the way it at first might seem. I did not meet a handsome stranger on the cruise. But there was a definite connection between the first time I ever treated myself to something totally fun, something that was, by my standards, even frivolous, and how Steve and I ended up saying our marriage vows.

I'll explain the connection in my next chapter, but first I must file a protest: I would not have even done such a thing if it hadn't been for three friends. So now I can blame them for encouraging me to spend that money I was always hoarding. One of my friends was a recently divorced single mom; one was a student like me, but a traditional student; and the other was a girl I worked with at Lone Star, a carefree spirit. We began to talk about how tired and burned out we were. I don't remember who suggested we go on a cruise, but we booked a seven-day Carnival Cruise Lines trip from San Juan to St. Thomas to St. Martin. I was such a travel novice. I was twenty-three and had gone nowhere but to New Hampshire and once to Michigan to visit Tim after he started his career as an engineer. I left Zackery and Trey with Grandma Linda and Granny, knowing they'd be safe and happy.

I had been casually dating a Stillwater friend, Ron, a single father raising his son. When I got back from the trip we continued dating, but the relationship was nothing serious. One thing that kept me from getting involved with him was that he and I had different ideas about what was important. He liked golf, but I couldn't have cared less about brand names. Ralph Lauren Polo shirts? Titleist golf balls? Big deal. Give me the Wal-Mart brand of both. Not for Ron, though—image was very important to him. We both recognized we weren't cut out for each other, but we remained friends and even babysat for each other when either of us would go out on dates.

Ron kept the boys one evening since I had a date in Tulsa. I had volunteered to take a neighbor's son into Tulsa since I was going there, anyway, but it turned out he couldn't leave until an hour and a half after I had already dropped off the boys, so I did something I had never done before.

Funny how the smallest events can turn out to be so significant. I went into a little bar in Stillwater near the campus, sat at the counter, and ordered a beer. Two guys were playing pool in the back and one of them came over to ask if I'd like to play. "I'm Steve, by the way," he said.

"I'm Lisa, but no, thanks, I'm only going to be here a little while longer." As I got up to leave, Steve came back and asked if he could walk me to my car.

"Sure," I said. He was nice looking and the gesture seemed innocent enough. By this time I had saved enough student loan money to buy a nice car. I paid cash for a Honda Civic and negotiated a great price, nearly fifty percent lower than the asking price.

I wonder what he thought when we got to the car and he saw the back seat loaded down with presents wrapped in Scooby Doo wrapping paper. I said quickly, "Those are for my son. He's turning three. I'm a single mother and I have another son, too. I have a date in Tulsa this evening and I need to get going."

He didn't hesitate. "If I give you my number, will you call me?

"Okay," I answered. But I didn't.

"I Take You, Steve," 1998

With such a hectic schedule, I forgot about the slip of paper Steve had given me. Two or three months went by, and one day as I was cleaning out my car console, I found his number. Oh well, I'll call him, I thought.

He didn't answer, so I left a message. He called me back and I wasn't home so *he* left a message. The pattern repeated itself until on the fourth time around we finally made contact. I found out he was a graduate student working on his PhD in wildlife and fisheries ecology. "But, Steve, I'm so busy. I'm trying to finish up my last credits and complete senior check-out, and I've got a lot of things going on," I explained when he asked me to go out with him.

"That's okay, Lisa, I'll call you again and we'll try to get together."

Well . . . it didn't seem like we were ever going to find a time when we were both free. He asked me, "Hey, Lisa, since your building and my building are right across the street, why don't we meet there for lunch if you have a few minutes?"

Sure, why not, I thought. It was no big deal. So why was I so nervous? "Les, do you think you could sit with me while I wait for this guy? He's a graduate student and he wants to meet me for lunch." I talked my friend Leslie into coming with me.

We ordered our food, Dutch treat of course, and sat down at one of the tables. "Oh, my God!" Leslie whispered. "He's so handsome. He looks like a movie star!" When she pointed it out, I realized that yes, he really was. He was tall and he had a clean, lean, look. "Listen, I have to go to poly sci," Leslie said. She left the two of us. I felt a little shy for some reason.

We sat and talked quite a while. He seemed interested in me as I told him about Zackery and Trey and the many things I was juggling. "They sound like good boys," he said. "You want to meet for lunch on Friday?" I agreed. We met at Red Lobster, and I insisted on paying for our meal. I guess I didn't want him to think it was a "date." Nor did I want him to think I was looking for a free meal. I wasn't ready, and to be even more specific, even though he was nice, I wasn't interested in adding another complication to my life.

Still, we continued to meet for lunch a few times. I think I must have told Steve everything there was to tell about my boys, and he always seemed interested, or at least the way he looked at me suggested he was.

One evening Steve called and Zackery answered the phone and said, "I know who you are, you're my mom's boyfriend." When I hung up the phone I said to Zackery, "I wished you hadn't said that. He really isn't my boyfriend." Zackery was doing a little dance and smiling saying over and over, "Mommy has a boyfriend, Mommy has a boyfriend. . ."

It wasn't until Steve came over one evening and I fixed dinner for him that we began to talk about something besides kids and school. My cruise album was laying on the end table and I asked him if he wanted to see the pictures. I went over each picture, telling him more about the scene shot. I went into a lot of detail about what we had seen and how much fun we had had.

"Wow, Lisa, this is a whole other side of you! I was beginning to wonder if you had any interests besides your boys! I was thinking we'd never get beyond those conversations. Much as they seem to be great kids . . . I mean, you have to do some other things, too."

Zackery came running out of the bedroom with his Scooby Doo pajamas and said, "I know who you are. You're my mommy's boyfriend and you keep leaving messages on the answering machine." We laughed and then came Trey, not far behind Zackery. Trey was holding his stuffed clown and sucking his thumb with the same hand. With the other hand, he was pointing at Steve, and then he crawled right up in Steve's lap. My heart sorta sank a bit and I whispered to Steve, "Is this okay?" We visited for a bit and then I excused myself and took the boys back to their bedroom, tucking them into their beds. I stayed with the boys for a while, as I didn't want them to think that I was choosing Steve over them. "Goodnight, sleep tight, and don't let the bed bugs bite," I said, giving them each a kiss. By the time I made it back to the living room Steve was ready to leave. He kissed my cheek, saying "Goodnight." I thought, well, I'm sure that's over.

Looking back, I wonder if his education intimidated me a little at first. Maybe that was the reason for the nonstop talking about my kids. I started to relax around him when I could tell he thought of me as interesting, and I was able to just be myself after that. We began talking about other things as the weeks passed. He told me about his privileged upbringing and I told him only some about mine, which was about as far away from his as it could be. Eventually I told him just about everything, even about my father and how fearful my mom was about him. He seemed to be in awe of the many challenges I had faced.

Later, he told me he loved me. Guarded, my reply was, "Why do you love me?"

He replied, "Lisa, I've never met anyone like you. I grew up with a silver spoon in my mouth and with opportunity in front of me, while you've had to create your own. You're such a good mom. You're a hard worker. You're smart, funny, and interesting. I respect you more than any person I've ever known." He told me he had about given up on me when we first started seeing each other because he thought I had no other interests besides my boys, and that seeing my pictures and hearing me describe the fun my friends and I had had on the cruise made him realize I was more than just a mom.

In early June 1998 Steve asked me to marry him. I was flabbergasted by his proposal, and the timing was unusual. My best friend since I was fourteen years old, Scott Alan Bowers, had been murdered when he refused to hand over his wallet during an armed robbery only days previous. Scott was thirty years old at the time of his death and I was twenty-four. Scott and I had been friends all those years and he had even taught me to drive his Jeep when I was only fourteen. I had ruined his transmission, but that didn't stop our friendship. He had a daughter, I had my two sons. We were inseparable as far as friends go. Steve proposed the evening I arrived back to Stillwater from Scott's funeral and I fell into his arms.

We married a few months later in October, two months prior to my college graduation. My mother's husband Dempsey was very generous with us. He gave us three thousand five hundred dollars so that we could have a big wedding if we wanted to, but whatever we decided, he said the money was our wedding gift.

I imagine it's no surprise to state that we decided to take that money along with an additional five thousand dollars that Steve's parents gave us and do the economical thing: We got married at the courthouse and had a small combined graduation and wedding party at our house. Always the frugal one, I talked him into us going in together to pay off his debts. I didn't have any debt other than my accumulated student loan money, again no surprise, but Steve had a lot of outstanding credit card bills. We started our married life with a clean slate.

And so now the connection between my first cruise with my two girl-friends and "Lisa Ditchkoff, Married Lady" becomes clear—the pictures I took on the cruise eventually led to Steve asking me to marry him.

MOMMY THE COLLEGE GRADUATE, 1998–2000

"At-Risk Youth." That was a description I could identify with. Maybe that's why my 1998 summer internship at Payne County Youth Services turned out to be unexpectedly rewarding. My family could have used services like what PCYS offered. I'm not sure we would have taken advantage of them, but we would have been good candidates for them, for sure. It's a nonprofit organization, and it offered, and still offers, its services at no charge.

The services at PCYS included counseling, foster care, and adoption programs, prevention, diversion, crisis intervention, parent education, victim's advocacy, workforce programming, emergency sheltering, and substance abuse treatment services. It offered mentors and educators in all those areas, and had a home visitation program for teenage parents. Was I uniquely suited for an internship program there? That answer is obvious.

I began my internship as an assistant in the teen parent family resource program. Later my responsibilities expanded to providing counseling and home visitations for teenage parents. I also helped coordinate educational and recreational activities. I became drawn to learn, asking a lot of questions about all the programs. I was aware of the irony of my involvement in those programs, but I was also confident that my life experiences had given me a special empathy for teens. I also realized once more how much I enjoyed planning group events. I would volunteer to organize them—no one even had to ask me. It was almost as if I were drawn to them.

"Lisa, how would you like to speak to a high school economics class?" My university-assigned supervisor stopped at the little interns' desk one afternoon as I was compiling the monthly activities schedule.

Omigosh, I'm so scared about speaking in front of a group! I thought, but I didn't say that. The only time I had tried, in my high school class as I gave a book report on Hitler, had been a failure. "Well . . . do you really think they'd want me to talk to them? What would I talk about?"

"It's a senior family planning class. You can share your experiences and what you learned from being such a young mother. I think your story would be really interesting to them. It might be a wake-up call for some of them, too."

My story? I didn't realize I had one. "Well, okay, I can try it. I've never done anything like that before. I'll try it, though."

I could hardly eat the morning before I spoke to those girls. I wrote out some notes and held onto them tightly as I was introduced by the teacher and went to the front of the room. I felt nauseated at even the thought of public speaking.

Here goes, I thought, as I stood up. "I'm Lisa. I am twenty-four years old, and I have two sons. One is eight years old and the other is four." Some of the girls' faces looked puzzled. "Yes, if you do the math, you'll figure out that I had my first baby when I was sixteen and my second when I was twenty, almost twenty-one. They have two different biological fathers, and I didn't marry either of them. I have one semester left before I graduate from OSU. I work at Payne County Youth Services, I clean a couple of houses in between classes, and I've been working one to three weekends a month at Lone Star Steakhouse in Tulsa for the past four years. I am here to tell you anything is possible if you want it enough. Well, let me take that line back and say 'everything is possible' if you want it enough and believe it enough.' Let me tell you a little more about how I ended up standing in front of you today. . ."

I then went into more detail about my story. As I told it, I realized two things. I actually had a story to tell. And I wasn't as fearful speaking to the class as I had thought I'd be. I continued talking and then answering questions afterwards.

I actually enjoyed myself just a little! But the experience went beyond enjoyment when a girl in the class came up to me afterwards. "Lisa, I have to tell you something. I'm pregnant. I was planning on having an abortion, but hearing you talk has changed my mind. I look at you and think, I can do it, and I don't have to give up my dreams."

I received an A in that internship requirement, and that left me only four courses to finish before I would receive my B.S. in December 1998. Steve continued to work toward his Ph.D. and I landed a position right out of college as a case manager with Big Brothers Big Sisters of Stillwater.

The timing was right for me to work full-time—Zackery was eight and Trey was four. We settled in to a more or less traditional family routine. Steve filed adoption papers for both boys, which eventually went through, so finally they had a father in more than just the biological sense. I also continued going back to Tulsa and working double shifts about one weekend a month and I continued cleaning a couple of houses in Stillwater. The money was too good to pass up and we needed it while Steve was in graduate school. We also needed a more dependable car so we were able to buy a brand new Ford Explorer.

What a time-tested, honorable program Big Brothers Big Sisters is! Once again, I was associated with an organization for which I felt a personal connection. I would look at those kids, so often left to fend for themselves as my brothers and I had been, and my heart would cry out to them. I learned to prepare monthly reports and files for a five-year accreditation audit, both of which became invaluable experiences later. I recruited and screened adult volunteers and matched children to each of them, and I conducted the required periodic evaluations. This part of my job was important to me and I spent a lot of time trying to make each match the best it could be. I remembered the tall, thin, self-conscious, and bored girl with broken teeth who used to hang out at a Tulsa park. I had needed an adult to take an interest in me. I didn't find any good role models or mentors until I went to work as a pregnant sixteen-year-old, and even at that, not a woman I could think of had ever said, "I want to be your friend. I believe in you. I support you." Somehow I had not fallen through the cracks completely, but I wanted to do what I could to build up the confidence and self-worth of the kids I saw every day so that maybe they'd avoid some of the cracks that had almost swallowed me. More than once I also got the opportunity to speak to high school classes or groups at the facility as I had done at PCYS. People often told me afterwards that my story had been helpful and even inspirational to them.

I also helped Big Brothers Big Sisters continue to help the kids by raising funds for the organization to stay afloat. When I heard about the need I said, "I'll do it!" I volunteered to take on an instrumental role in the Stillwater center's annual "Bowl for Kids' Sake" event for two years in a row. Sadly, I noticed that matching those children with disabilities was a tougher challenge. Most of the time, they were never matched. Seeing the need for providing more opportunities to these children, I also offered to coordinate all the group activities monthly rather than the previous every-other-month-or-so schedule and found funding opportunities so the agency was expense-free for every event. The kids loved the activities with their mentors and it gave those children that weren't yet matched an opportunity to have something to do. And once again I felt a special "aliveness" as I organized the fundraiser and viewed firsthand its success. Getting people together, organizing ways to allow them to interact, being in the middle of all that socializing and schmoozing for a cause—those activities were becoming my forte.

I loved being in the center of action. The aliveness didn't just come from working with people, though. There was something about doing a good turn to someone else that also made me feel like I was doing something worthwhile. Maybe my motives weren't completely pure—after all, I got some personal satisfaction when I saw my influence on a child or coworker had made that person's day happier. But I did recognize two things: I loved being in charge, and I loved helping and nurturing people, for whatever the reasons.

Maybe that's why I wanted to be so involved in Zackery's and Trey's lives. Maybe that desire to mold another life was now ready to take wings, moving beyond my immediate family to the needs of others, and when I saw an opportunity to do that I gravitated towards it. Ultimately, did it matter why I did those things? I don't think it *did* matter, and I don't think it *does* matter. It's just me.

Truth was, though, it wasn't just me. I realize now it was in my genes. The debate about heredity vs. environment is far from being settled. I never took a course in genetics, but I did know this even then: I was different in so many ways from the family members I knew. My mother was, and is, an introvert, very calm, quiet, always dependent on her man, content with just living day to day and not rocking the boat. She was as laid-back as I was driven. Were my ambitiousness, extroverted personality, and need to nurture just reactions against how I was brought up?

Or was there another explanation? The questions about my identity were forming in my mind. It wouldn't happen right away, but a shattering experience down the road would be the catalyst for me to seek answers to questions.

BYE, STILLWATER AND HELLO, AUBURN

Everyone should have the opportunity to go to an Auburn University football game once in their life. When we moved to Auburn in January 2001, it wasn't long before we were caught up in the excitement of the SEC and its rivalries. It was impossible not to feel the enthusiasm, and it was contagious.

The first Auburn University football game was indeed an eye opening energetic and eventful experience. First, I never imagined having to park a mile or so away from the stadium. Walking towards the stadium was an awesome experience in its own right. The people chanting "War Eagle!" the food, the excitement, were all part of a culture. Then in the stadium people were roaring with enthusiasm for their beloved AU Tigers.

The city of Auburn loves its football and it also takes its AU Tigers football seriously, but, some would argue convincingly, not half as seriously as the university itself. Case in point: In October 2008 Coach Tommy Tuberville fired Offensive Coordinator Tony Franklin, hired by Tuberville himself at the end of the 2007 season, after only six games. The straw that broke the Tigers' back was the loss to Vanderbilt on October 4, 2008. Vanderbilt? A top-drawer university with a bottom-drawer football team? Tony Franklin was gone within a couple of days.

Then the Tigers roared again and Tommy Tuberville himself was history in December, after the rest of the season resulted in only one win out of the remaining seven games. It didn't matter what his previous record had been. Tuberville had been at Auburn since 1999. He had led AU to the most wins in school history, the Sugar Bowl title and its first SEC Championship,

SEC Western Division titles, and eight consecutive bowl appearances. But none of those past accomplishments saved him from being blamed for a dismal 2008 season in which Auburn suffered the humiliation of being defeated by its archrival, University of Alabama's Crimson Tide.

Auburn, Alabama is a relatively small city of about 55,000 people in eastern Alabama about 100 miles from Atlanta to the east and about 145 miles from Birmingham, which is directly west. It's a college town–AU is its claim to fame. AU's own claims to fame center around the sciences, agriculture, and its engineering schools.

Auburn became our new home in early January 2001 when Steve, newly embossed Ph.D. in hand, landed a job as an assistant professor of wildlife ecology and management in Auburn's renowned School of Forestry and Wildlife Management. It was quite an offer and we knew it.

Since both Zack (he insisted he wanted to be called "Zack," not Zackery) and Trey were in elementary school, I applied right away at the university and was put to work through TES (Temporary Employment Services), where I floated around various departments. I did a variety of paperwork duties, most of which would fall under the job description of "Administrative Assistant." Most of the tasks were not what I would have chosen as my ideal ways to use my education and talents, and some were downright boring, not the challenges I was used to, but I learned a lot of ins-and-outs of organization, supervision, and management, and I met some wonderful people from departments campus-wide. I would eventually be grateful for the skills I learned and the relationships I made.

In 2001 my experience coordinating training sessions for one of my temporary assignments landed me a new job at the AU Hotel and Dixon Conference Center. The only opening was a secretarial position that I took with the expectation that I could become a conference service manager when a position opened, which happened within a couple of weeks after I started there.

I loved the work and I took great pride in my job. One thing that gave me great satisfaction was increasing sales. For example, I found I could convince a conference coordinator to upgrade the conference's banquet meals by adding appetizers or upgrading the dessert.

I did *not* love the fact that when I arrived about 5:30 a.m. on the day of a scheduled 7:30 a.m. meeting, the room would usually not be ready. A meeting might be scheduled to start in an hour and nothing had been done to set up the room, so I found myself vacuuming, locating A/V equipment, moving tables, and running around in a near panic to do what should have been done the night before or at least before I arrived. It wasn't exactly the housekeeping chores I hated, it was the fact that I had promised my customers we would have their room ready so they could start on time and it wasn't. Though the hotel had recently separated from its former relationship under university management, which resulted in a large number of employees securing positions primarily at the university, the lackadaisical attitude at the hotel at that time, which seemed to me to come down from the top, bothered me more and more.

Weeks passed and the end of my ninety-day probation period was approaching. I had been telling my supervisor, "This isn't right. I come in at 7:00 and everything should be ready. Instead, I'm coming in at 5:30 a.m.

knowing that there's work that needs to be done. I'm having to take off my suit coat and vacuum. Nothing is set up. I am finding myself working sixty or seventy hours a week. My husband and children need me."

My review day arrived. "Lisa, we're going to offer you a thirty percent raise. In addition, we are going to add a commission to your sales." The hotel manager added, "We want to keep you. How does this sound?"

I would be making more than Steve was! "Pretty good, actually. I'll give it a try," I said.

Which is what I did. But it didn't take me long to face reality: I felt like the new position allowed the management to take advantage of me. The truth was, I had been given a raise so I could pretend I was happy. A probationary period is not only for the employer but for the employee, I realized. And more money didn't mean more happiness. Things didn't much change except I was given more files and more work resulting in working even longer hours. One Sunday before leaving for work, Zack looked up at me and said, "Mom, it's Sunday, you're working again?" I couldn't get the look on his face or the tone in his voice off my mind.

The next day I brought in my resignation letter early in the morning. A dear little banquets worker there who had worked at the conference center for several years was vacuuming the conference room, having arrived early to assure everything was as it should be. I had gotten to know her and she had risen to the occasion for me several times as much as her heavy work load allowed when I was overwhelmed. Ester didn't have to be there as early as she was and my guess is she probably didn't even clock in. Looking back, I think now that she came in early just to help alleviate my stress level.

"Ester, I have to show you something." I handed her the letter and as she read it she started crying.

"Lisa, you are the only person here who has ever treated us with respect."

Was I such a wonderful person? It was not that at all. The fact was, I had worn shoes not much different from hers. In a people-centered, service industry job, I knew from experience that it is as important to get along well with your coworkers as it is to treat your customers well. I also believed in treating every person with respect regardless of their position, education level, the salary they earn, and their ethnicity. The bosses I had had who had praised me and acted as if they valued me had made me work harder and better for them. I will never forget Ester's comments as she wiped her teary eyes.

The people . . . arranging events for them . . . overseeing others' work in a way that made sure every detail was handled properly and in advance . . . taking pride in the smooth and hitch-free outcome . . . those were the things I enjoyed. An idea was slowly taking form in my mind. My spirit was saying to me, start your own event planning service business, Lisa. There are more than enough potential clients in this city and in neighboring Opelika for you to succeed.

The idea began to grow. I didn't act upon it, though, not yet. Meanwhile I arrived back at TES working various secretarial positions until I started a position as a planning coordinator for the AU Center for Children, Youth and Families, under the College of Human Sciences. This position was more suited to my degree in family relations and child development and much of what I did again became close to my heart.

My biggest responsibility was recruitment of advanced scholars from minority racial groups and of junior faculty for a workshop that was designed to enhance diversity through mentoring and collaboration. I was also responsible for the resubmission of the grant titled "Auburn University's Children's Research Center" to the National Science Foundation. All important and meaningful concerns, and I was proud to take my part. The position I was in was created for me for a short period of time, but was long-term dependent upon securing the center grant. I did a lot of research on the west counties of Alabama, often referred to as the "Black Belt." The statistics were some of the worst I had ever heard. A whopping *one hundred percent* of children in some schools were on free and reduced lunch programs, and the area had the highest percentage of teen pregnancy in the state. Not to mention many cases of abuse and neglect. My heart ached for such a need and I became even more emotionally invested in the concept of developing this national children's research center.

My fellow employees in the College of Human Sciences at Auburn University were congenial and I grew to respect and develop friendships with many of them. One woman in the department, in particular, Dale Downing, did everything assigned to her with special competence. I admired her initiative and work ethic and became good friends with her. Fast forward twelve years, and she is still near and dear to me. Dale, among other close friends, has helped mold me into the woman I am today.

I cherish one of my best friendships from 2001 to today. The story goes like this: While working one of my temporary employee positions at Auburn, a group of women invited me to lunch. During that lunch, the topic of conversation was Andrea, a fellow co-worker. I didn't participate in the shallow talk about Andrea; rather I talked about things and places and the wonderful food. I thought to myself that night, Hmmm . . . Andrea is absolutely beautiful. She's stylish in her daily dress, she works out every morning, she's in a position which involves confidential information, and her pay is probably more than other administrative positions pay.

So I continued thinking. Someone who is not as physically fit (or just plain "out of shape"), someone who doesn't care for herself physically the way Andrea does, someone who doesn't receive as much pay or maybe isn't as pretty, someone who is also insecure about herself, would probably be threatened or perhaps jealous of her. So the next day, as I was walking the halls speaking to everyone and saying "hello," I stopped and invited Andrea to lunch. She accepted, and we had a marvelous meal and conversation. We've been friends since and I'm so glad I didn't listen to those other women regarding Andrea. Otherwise, I would have been just as guilty at judging as they are.

While Andrea and I were getting pedicures together one day, the cute Asian girl working on my feet said, "You need a eyebrow." I exclaimed that I get a rash when I have an eyebrow waxing. She again insisted, "You need a eyebrow! You have bushy busy eyebrow. You need a eyebrow!" Andrea and I were laughing hysterically and I said, "Oh no, men tell me they like my eyebrows." In a very serious voice, this petite Asian woman said, while her hand was motioning back and forth as if giving a child a scolding saying "no, no", says, "Oh no! You never listen to what men have to say. They never tell you the trufth!" Andrea and I couldn't stop laughing. My eyebrows were even mentioned specifically once in a poem that was written for me. How often does a woman have a poem written about her that specifically mentions her eyebrows?

I do admit that Andrea and a few friends of mine laughed about the poem often and still do. Surrounding myself with positive people is important to me, and they remind me that you can't allow yourself to accept the judgment of yourself by others. An article I read a while back called "Living the Hi-Def Life" offers some advice: "Be willing to live an uncommon life and not be dissuaded by the thousands of low-definition lives that will surround you."[9]

[9]From *Homelife*, online version, http://www.homelife-digital.com, Lifeway Christian Resources, Nashville, TN, August 29, 2008.

CHASING ANOTHER DREAM

By 2002, Steve and I were both well integrated into the culture and so-cial life of Auburn and the university. Zack was twelve and Trey was eight, both with lots of friends and activities. Some of my happiest memories of the years when I had been about Zack's age centered around those summer weeks at Nana's and Papa's vacation cottage in New Hampshire, and I wanted the boys to make their own carefree summer memories.

Ever the financial organizer and tightwad, I had told Steve in 2002 that within two years we would own a lake property. Ever the realist, Steve had said, "No way. We'll never be able to afford it, Lisa. You're out of your mind!" This was about a year after we purchased our home.

Not long after I set this goal, during Zack's soccer team party having casual conversation and told a lovely man with a Greek accent, a local de-veloper, that I wanted to find a lake property.

"You want lake property? I show you lake property," Chris Koullas said.

The property was on Lake Martin. We drove to it right away. On it stood an old, rickety, outdated 535 square foot house trailer. But it had lake frontage, and we could dock a boat.

I convinced Steve that if we found we couldn't afford the payments, we could sell it and make an immediate profit. I already knew this because I had been researching property on Lake Martin and was familiar with the prices there. I knew we could make at least a thirty thousand dollar profit without even doing anything to improve it. What a great opportunity! I told Nana about finding the property and how I was so excited that we would be able to provide cottage type experiences for Zack and Trey. Nana called me later and said, "Papa and I want to help you with a down payment."

I started crying. I couldn't believe it. There sat a dream and it became a reality. Zack and Trey took to the property like fish take to water. I could still not believe our good fortune. Steve's parents brought the boat he had grown up with down to us and we began dreaming about eventually building a cabin on the property.

And yet, something fundamental was absent. I was very happy with the status quo and I wasn't an unhappy person in general, so it wasn't exactly that something was lacking—it was more that it just wasn't there. What was it?

Well, one dream of owning a lake property had become a reality, but I had another dream, a more life-changing one. That was the dream that was missing. I didn't realize it, though, until a family tragedy became the impetus for me to find that dream and act on it.

SCOTTY, MY CHEERLEADER, 2003

"Hi, again, little sister. How ya doin'? I'm kinda bored here and wanna know if it's okay for me to come to Auburn." Scotty again, for the third time that day. Mom had gotten him a calling card so he could place long distance calls, and he certainly made good use of it. I didn't mind, though. He was such a gentle man. He was generous to a fault. If you made a complimentary comment about something he owned, his watch, for instance, he'd say, "You can have it. It's yours." And he wasn't kidding. He would nearly force you to take it.

His frequent questions about our father—who he was, where he was, what kind of man he was, what new information, if any, our mother knew about him—had made my curiosity grow over the years. And when I had Zack and later Trey, I would look at them and wonder who they looked like.

Maybe Scotty was revealing something about himself when he threw that brick labeled with his name in the restaurant window. Maybe he was saying, "Hey, I'm here! I'm a person! I'm Scott Connor!" Could he have been looking for himself, calling out to the world to tell him who he was and where he came from? He didn't look like his mother or have a personality like hers. So who did he take after? Maybe he wanted to know his roots so he could understand himself better and fill in the gaps. I don't know. Obviously my training is not in psychology, even though one course was a requirement, but these thoughts make sense to me.

In some ways Scotty and I were very different in how we dealt with our misshapen family tree, which was lopped off on one side as if there had been a canker or a disease that destroyed half of it. He wanted to find the missing branches. I thought about them but instead of obsessing about them, I just forged my own identity and planted my own new family tree with Zack, Trey, and Steve. Or so I thought, not knowing that many of my personality traits and ways of dealing with the world had come not just from the Zerveskes roots but from the Connor(s) ones.

Scotty was a resident of the state mental institution in Venita for seven years. After many experimental drugs were tried on him, one finally worked, and the hospital released him to an assisted living facility for mental patients. He did well there, though he could not travel alone.

Scotty loved Auburn football. He followed it in Oklahoma and he was thrilled to be able to go to Jordan-Hare Stadium. Mom and Dempsey picked him up a couple of times in Venita and she and Scotty came to Auburn together. He went to two or three games. The first year he and Steve sat in the stadium, rain pouring down on them, watching the drizzle-soaked Tigers slog through the four quarters. Steve told me later that in spite of the weather, Scotty had had the time of his life. He enjoyed a hot dog and slurped a soft drink, the simple things we often take for granted.

In the fall of 2003, Scotty got a routine checkup and found out something that scared him. His doctor had diagnosed an extraordinarily low heart rate, a probable side effect of all the experimental medications he had taken over the years. "Doc says I need a pacemaker immediately. I told the Doc that I had to go visit my little sister in Auburn and that I wanted to go to another Auburn game. I know I am going to die," Scotty said.

"No you're not. Nana has a pacemaker and she's fine," I insisted.

"Really, I know it, I know I am going to die and I have to come see you."

"Okay, of course, come on," I said. I would never turn him away, though I thought he was letting his imagination run a little too wild.

Mom once again brought him down to Auburn. Scotty and I went to the mall together because I had a job interview at AU for a higher position in the Development Office and I needed new shoes. We had a low-key, easy, brother-and-sister afternoon. He sat patiently while I tried on dressy shoes.

I guess I might say I have good taste—just not the money to indulge it. I tried on an expensive pair that I loved, but the price tag made me say, "I can't justify buying these." This may have been my first experience buying myself something I loved that was a full price item.

In the gentle, encouraging way he always had, he said, "Oh, go ahead, little sister. They look great and you need something good to wear to the interview. You work hard and you deserve them!" Well, he talked me into them, though I guess shoes weren't enough to get me hired for that job. I didn't get it. In fact, I applied for several jobs and didn't get one of them in Development. The Dean of Architecture Design and Construction whom I had met with about his vacant position later told me that the VP of Development at the time told him that I wasn't qualified and he questioned my "monotonous background." I asked Dean Bennett, "Are you sure he said 'monotonous'?"

Monotonous? Hmmm, I thought. I would never have thought that about myself. I hand delivered some paperwork across campus to Alabama Cooperative Extension System and ran into the director, Gaines Smith. "Hey, Gaines, How are you today? Someone just told me that I was *monotonous*. That means "dull and boring," right?

Gaines replied, "Yes, that's right," as he shook his head and chuckled softly. Later I even looked up the actual definition of the word just to assure I had the meaning right. I still couldn't believe it. I guess this goes to show that people form opinions and judge others without really knowing them.

I had taken off work a couple of days to be with Scotty. During that time together in 2003 I shared my dream of starting my own events planning service business as a stepping stone to eventually owning a unique venue. We talked about it quite a while. I also talked about my knack for fund raising and how ultimately I could see helping nonprofit organizations with fund raising events. I had actually stepped out on my own already and done a couple of events, prepping and planning during lunch and using some vacation time, so I already had two clients, if I wanted to continue down that path.

Always the cheerleader, Scotty insisted, "Little sister, I think you should do it. You'll do great. You need to do this." He repeated the same theme over and over with variations.

The night before the game I sat on the porch with Scotty and Mom, who had gone outside to smoke. Mom, Scotty, and I sat listening to the sounds of autumn—the frogs croaking from a nearby pond, the cicadas' high-speed clickety whirr. They live such a short time, I thought. They'll be gone soon. And yet they sound as if they can keep on clicking and whirring forever.

"I'm going to die," Scotty said.

Both Mom and I said almost the same words, right away. "Oh, no, Scotty. Nana has a pacemaker and she's done fine for many years."

"No, you don't understand. I know I'm going to die and I don't want to do this. I know I'm going to die."

"But you'll die if you don't, Scott." I'm not sure who said that, but it was true. Without the pacemaker he had no chance of living to old age.

We visited Trey during lunch at his elementary school and after drove out to our property at Lake Martin. Sitting on the porch swing, Scotty said, "I'd love to go for a boat ride." The water level had dropped at the lake and our boat was in storage. So, I dragged the old aluminum fishing boat out from underneath the lake trailer along with the trolling motor, paddles, and three life jackets. "Come on, let's get in", I said. Both Mom and Scott exclaimed, "There's no way we're going in that boat!" I insisted and off we went with Rock, our dog, riding shotgun. We travelled out a good ways on the water and the juice ran out. Fortunately, we did have paddles.

We all had a wonderful time on that visit. Mom took Scott back to Venita. Only two weeks after his pacemaker was installed, he collapsed of a massive heart attack. By the time the ambulance arrived, it was too late and he died quickly. None of us was able to get to him in time. Scott Connor was thirty-two years old.

Scotty and me. This was the last picture taken of him before he passed away.

SAYING GOODBYE TO A BROTHER WITH A HEART OF GOLD

I was working on my Christmas cards, early in fact, when I found out. Not knowing the terrible news yet, I called to talk to Mom, forgetting that she had traveled out of state with her girlfriend for a wedding. Dempsey answered.

"Hi, Dempsey. I'm just calling to get an address for a Christmas card."

He replied, "Scotty died." I couldn't believe it. I didn't want to believe it. My heart sank to my stomach. I had talked to Scotty just the night before. He had been very tired and out of breath, more so than usual, but I thought he was going to be okay.

I hung up the phone and said to Steve, "Scotty died."

"When it's your time, it's your time," Steve replied.

I told him we needed to leave for Tulsa right away. "The boys can stay in Auburn with me and you can go," Steve said.

I couldn't even believe what I had just heard. I said, "These boys were close to my brother and my brother was close to them. We'll be leaving the house in one hour and I hope you will go with us." The boys and I packed up quickly and finally Steve did make the decision to come. The funeral was in Tulsa. Mom, Dempsey, and I planned the funeral together. We selected the theme "A Heart of Gold," and we chose the flowers, the music, and made all the arrangements.

There were only about twenty-five people there, some of them friends of my mother's from her work, a couple of my friends, a couple of people from the facility where Scotty had lived, and one long-time friend of Scotty's. I felt so sad looking around at the small group of people who were there to celebrate Scotty's life.

Get an illness like Scotty's and you'll see people abandon you, too, I thought. People shy away from the mentally ill. Scotty had lost most of his friends years ago. Only one had stood by him, Brandon "Brandy" Jenkins, a guitarist and singer from Tulsa and a friend of Scotty's for years. For a while he and Scotty had been roommates. Brandy was living in Texas by this time. I was always so proud of Brandy. As his performing career accelerated with recorded albums, accolades, and regular gigs, he never became too big to continue his friendship with Scotty. When Scotty was committed, Brandy would come to Venita, pick him up, take him to lunch, and bring him back to the facility. Brandy came to the funeral, guitar in hand, planning to sing. But he couldn't do it—his emotions got the better of him. So we played a CD of his music. Brandy was a true friend and I will always respect him for that.

My mom was very quiet as she sat there with tears flowing down her face. My cries were very deep, with a feeling of tightness in my stomach as I gasped for air. Tim also came for the funeral, very sad at the loss of his brother.

Such a subdued and low-key send-off for a once exuberant and lively boy who had become a gentle, generous man. He had encouraged me to follow my dream. I couldn't put his pep talks out of my mind.

Scotty, I wish you knew: I did what you kept telling me to do. We got back to Auburn and I took the next few days off work, mostly staying home alone listening to Brandy's CD of the songs we had played at the funeral. The following Friday I met with an attorney, Jim McLaughlin. I had the plans mapped out in my mind. Jim and I legalized and formalized the business, and then the attorney and I had a more casual conversation.

"Lisa, you know you might want to go talk to Ron Anders, who owns Anders Bookstore. The City of Auburn has this big sporting event coming up next year and Ron is in charge of it and, between you and me, Ron could use some help."

I went from the attorney's office straight to the bookstore. I told Ron, "I just started a new event planning business and the company also includes fund raising. I'd like to help you with your event."

I got the contract. Technically, this was my third official client since I had secured two others before finalizing the new business plan. Handling the details of the plan of action with Ron and local attorney Rick Davidson, who served as co-chair, was a learning experience that took a little time, but we worked together well and my involvement with that event immediately put me in direct personal contact with Auburn's "A List," the CEOs, the general managers, the city planners, and the other influential people of the community.

So PEPS—Professional Event Planning Services, LLC was born. The next month, I resigned from my AU job. By this time, though, my original position in the department had changed several times due to instability of funding. It wasn't until three months after my resignation that I actually left the university and was full-time with PEPS. Soon after I got started, I knew I'd need help with the administrative end of the business, and I hired my friend and colleague Dale as my assistant. When I was too busy to handle all of the details, I called on her to help. After about a year, I was able to hire her full-time. She and I worked out of either her house or mine. Many of our coworkers, the professors, and the staff in the College of Human Sciences already knew of my first steps into event planning and they had offered their encouragement to both of us. Dale's been with me ever since that beginning. I would bet that few people are as blessed as me to have an assistant like Dale, a dear friend and a phenomenal employee.

I had an interesting meeting not long after I left the university with the VP for Development, Bob McGinnis. As we sat talking over a meal, he explained, "Lisa, there's something I want you to understand about yourself. You're very pretty, you're very smart, you have extremely strong work ethics, and because you're who you are you're a threat to a lot of people. In fact, you're a threat to all of my employees except two. And, because you're a threat, they will say things about you that aren't true."

I explained how I was confused by what he telling me. "Lisa, you are doing exactly what you need to do. You needed the opportunity to spread your wings and fly," he said. So that explains why I didn't get one of those jobs, I guess. It was very confusing for me to understand. During the transitional time of departing AU and developing PEPS, I continued thinking about what Bob had said.

Zack and Trey had a Space Jam CD that I knew pretty well so I listened to Seal's version of the song *I Believe I Can Fly*. I must have listened to that song fifty times. Here are some of the lyrics:

I Believe I Can Fly

I'm leaning on the everlasting arms

If I can see it, then I can do it

If I just believe it, there's nothing to it

I believed that no matter what, as long as I believe in myself, everything truly is possible.

Busy as Steve was with developing a reputation for his research and other aspects of his own academic career, he was supportive, as well, though the demands of building the business and my involvement in Zack's and Trey's school and sports activities left us little time to work on our relationship—to talk, to have fun, to just be with each other. Each of us was very focused, though maybe not as much as we should have been on each other.

"Working 9 to 5, what a way to make a living." Neither of us had that kind of job. Pushing papers, filing folders, or keeping the books for someone else in an office all day was just not for me. I had tried it. I found out quickly that working 9:00 a.m. to 5:00 p.m. as a business owner was not going to be in the stars for a long while, if ever. Steve's drive was equally intense, as he was hoping to receive tenure in three years compared to most professors, who take five years.

I was in my element making connections, schmoozing, and in a real way helping people achieve something they needed to do for their business or organization. Being so interconnected with Auburn's and Opelika's prominent citizens also gave me some opportunities to participate in meeting other kinds of needs.

For example, I took on the planning role for the Auburn Football Lettermen Club in 2004, which in 2007 held a combination twenty-fifth anniversary celebration and fundraiser in honor of Lee Carpenter, a former AU defensive back who was stricken in 1986 with Lou Gehrig's disease. We hosted a Lee Carpenter Golf Tournament and a dinner sponsored by Coach Pat Dye, and the next day enjoyed an AU scrimmage and lunch at Jordan-Hare Stadium.

On occasion I still read the press release my office prepared from that 2007 event:

> This anniversary celebration/fundraiser for Lee Carpenter is the story of the qualities that make us successful members of a team, community, or family—relationships,

shared experiences, generosity, love, faith, hope, teamwork and overcoming adversity whether in life or on the football field.

Auburn itself was a kind of family, and I felt myself a part of it through my involvement with the Auburn Football Lettermen Club. In preparation for this event, I gathered research about Lee, going back to when he was diagnosed. The following is a quote from an article in the Birmingham Post Herald, October 7, 1996:

> Lee Carpenter never asked for worldly success and he didn't get it. . . ALS hasn't closed doors for him. Instead, it's opened new doors to people's hearts and put the value of his life in a whole new light. Lee Carpenter's story isn't one of pity, greed or anger. It isn't even a story about one man. Instead, it is a story about faith, family, friends, and football—four cornerstones of life in Alabama.

I think Lee Carpenter may be the longest living ALS patient. What a blessing to have this family in my life. Lee is just one of the many people I've been blessed to know since the founding of PEPS. So many stories have touched my heart.

I have a great story about the first time legendary former football coach Pat Dye and I met. One of my biggest pet peeves is being late. I couldn't find a parking spot at the Auburn University Beard Eaves Coliseum. By the time

I parked, I was already a few minutes late so I was running, literally, through the halls looking for Coach Dye's office. Finally, I found it. Coach and I sat for two-and-a-half hours chatting. Even though I'm a talker, he actually did most of the talking, sharing his life stories. Later he invited me out to his place, where several former football players were gathering for a hunt. Coach drove me around his hunting camp. We got out and walked around. Still, he was doing most of the talking. As we headed back to his truck he said, "Lisa, I understand how you got from Oklahoma to Auburn but explain how you got from Boston to Oklahoma."

I replied, "Coach I don't know you well enough to trust you with my story." He just looked at me, got into the truck, looked at me again, and we drove off. I think Coach respected me right away.

I loved my business and the opportunities to be of help that stemmed from my event planning activities. Yet I knew myself well enough to recognize that I had to have a continually modified list of challenges, and a new one, a potentially life-changing one, was taking shape in my mind.

"Maybe You Should Think about Moving Back There," 2004

As usual, once I got an idea in my mind, it became a determination. I was going to track down the father that Scotty had wanted so much to find.

Nana and I had always talked a lot by telephone, especially during those years I was in college at OSU. Mom had told Nana that when she and Papa died, she would not come to their funerals due to deaths being public knowledge and because of her fears of my father. Her fears stemmed not just from my father alone, but from those he was connected to. Through the grapevine she was sure Tommy would find out and come looking for her, looking for us. Nana was truly devastated. Papa was, too. Nana had always been a worrier and this was something that worried the dickens out of her. She called me several times crying.

That's it, I said to myself. It was time to come out of twenty-seven years of involuntary hiding. More importantly, though, I wanted to help my mom overcome her years of fear, if possible. She had been paralyzed by her fear all of the years I remember. She looked over her shoulder before getting in the car and always locked the door immediately after. She never had a checking account, as she was afraid of paper trails. She was afraid to get a credit card, afraid to put gas in a car, afraid to drive on a highway, afraid, afraid, afraid . . .

So sad and crippling to live every day in fear. I wanted to help my mom, and I knew that her parents might soon need her help, as they were dealing with some of the health problems that afflict older people. I wanted her to get over her fears enough to be able to go to Boston if she had to.

JUST A FEW OF MY FORMER AU FOOTBALL PLAYER FRIENDS.

Jackie Burkett and me. Jackie referred to this picture as "beauty and the beast."

Tom and Mary Lynn Bryan, and me.

Jeremy Ingle and me.

Love you, Kess Fabian! Kess is an honorary member of the AFLC.

"My Rock" Haven Fields and me.

Thom Gossom, Jr. and me. Visit Actor/Writer's website: www.bestgurl.com.

James "Big O" Owens and me during one of our visits in his home. I'm holding a "Letterman of the Year Award" given to him a couple of years prior.

With Al Del Greco.

With Antarrious "A.T." Williams.

BC & Cynthia Campbell said, "You love us and we love you!" BC is an honorary member of the AFLC.

Ken Rice, "A True Auburn Tiger," and me.

Terry Henley and me.

With Tim Wood and Rick Westbrook.

I asked myself, is anything truly possible? Yes, everything is possible. I needed to get to Southie. An opportunity to go there came earlier than I had expected.

"Mom, have you heard from Nana and Papa?"

"God, yes. They're onto each other all the time and Papa tells me Ma is showing some dementia. She shouldn't be driving anymore. He says you wouldn't want to be in the car when she drives, if that's what you call running through stop signs like they're not even there. She even dozed at the wheel while at a stop and then put her foot on the gas instead of the brakes."

"Maybe you should think about moving back there, Mom."

"There's no way in hell, Lisa . . ."

It was the summer of 2004. It seemed like a good time to try to convince her to go to Southie. Her parents needed her. Nana had come once or twice to Tulsa when we were kids, but she had decided she was too old to travel so there was no other way to assess Nana's mental state unless my mother saw it for herself. Besides, Mom was thinking of retiring from her job, and she needed something to occupy her mind and her time, or at least I thought she did. I don't think she agreed with me . . . but I did talk her into making a trip if I agreed to join her there.

It was a huge step for her. She told me several times that she was afraid of accidentally running into Tommy. Still, she let me make her a reservation. Steve took over the chauffeuring duties for all Zack's and Trey's sports and school activities while I was gone.

I packed my bags and drove to Atlanta's Hartsfield-Jackson airport on a warm summer day in June 2004. Mom had already arrived in Southie. I wondered what kinds of drama this reunion might create.

My Nana's 80th birthday. My two cousins walked her down the aisle and crowned her. I wouldn't have missed it for anything.

My Papa wearing a couple of his presents from his 90th birthday. I wouldn't have missed it for anything.

The Return to Southie, 2004

A Starbucks latte was beside me in the cup holder as I drove. It wasn't too often that I would spend the money on one but this was a special occasion. I hated the thought that Nana and Papa were getting too old to take care of themselves. But we had to be honest when we examined their circumstances and be realistic about their future.

Girl, you've done a lotta livin' for someone only thirty years old, I thought. What kind of life had my father had? I knew almost nothing about Southie or about the man we had run away from. I could barely remember leaving our flat on Peter Street, and my memories of anyone called "Dad" were so vague that I wasn't even sure they were real.

"You're so beautiful." I remembered those three words and I thought my dad had said them to me, but I had no way to know for sure. "I am going to find out if he can be located in South Boston anywhere," I promised myself. I needed to find him. For myself, sure—but even more than that, it was time to help my mother reconcile with him in some way so she will no longer be living in the fear she had lived with for so many years.

The next few hours were routine. Mainly, I thumbed through a *People* magazine while I carried on a conversation with an older man in a suit who sat next to me. His flight had originated in Dallas, where he had been on business, and he was returning to Boston, where he was CEO of a brokerage firm. He was surprised to find out I had been born in Southie. "But your accent—it sounds Southern," he commented. "And you don't look Irish." I explained that my father was Irish-American but my mom was from Lithuanian background. I told him I really thought of myself as a Southerner since I had lived in the South most of my life.

"So what do you know about South Boston?" I asked him. He told me everyone who had lived in Boston for any length of time knew it was a haven for what Bostonians called "The Irish Mafia." It had always been that way. He remembered his father, who had been in the concrete business, talking about thugs from Southie trying to shake him down years ago. The FBI had conducted a huge sting a few years back, he said, and a lot of those creeps had been rounded up and had done time.

"Would I know the names of any of them?" I asked.

"Probably not, unless you've heard of a guy named James Bulger. They called him 'Whitey' on the streets because of his light hair and complexion. He was a cold-blooded killer. They never caught him. He's on the lam somewhere."

I knew that name. I had heard my mother mention it once. Maybe that was enough information for me to pump from this guy. The rest of the flight we talked about inconsequential things. He suggested tourist sites to take in. "The bar where they supposedly filmed *Cheers* is a waste," he told me. "Everyone's always disappointed when they go looking for it. But you have to eat some clams down at the harbor when you're here. Not far from South Boston there's a place called The Clam Box. If you like history, there's an old fort on Castle Island at the end of Carson Beach." I knew of Castle Island because that had been Nana and Papa's regular hangout when the weather was good.

Our conversation came to a stop as a flight attendant announced, "Ladies and gentlemen, the captain has turned on the seatbelt sign. Please return to your seats and fasten your seatbelts in preparation for landing. We should touch down in a few moments. Welcome to Boston."

I picked up my luggage and hailed a taxi to South Boston, giving the driver Nana's and Papa's address. I had known the address by heart for years as I often sent cards, letters, and pictures of the boys.

I left the windows down in the taxi. The cool breeze feels good, I thought. I noticed that the trees were leafy, some of them in bloom, contrasting with the drabness of the neighborhoods we passed through. I was fascinated with the narrow streets the cab driver was navigating and the mostly narrow, three-story homes and apartments, built almost on top of each other. Some were clapboard, some were brick, some had shingled siding. They looked old to me. Many had a small front porch. Occasionally I spotted one that had obviously been renovated on the outside with new vinyl siding, gutters, and shutters. Many were in obvious need of a little TLC. A few of them had yards about the size of a picnic blanket. The back yards I could see were narrow and not much larger. Very few had more than one tree, though some of the trees were big enough to practically fill the yard. Very few had garages and those that did had the garages constructed underneath the building or built as a separate building for one car in the back of the house. Houses with garages are a luxury in South Boston. I knew Papa and Nana had one and that they also had an apartment underneath their own flat that they rented out. Though they were not rich, the garage showed their affluence relative to many other people in Southie.

As we turned onto Broadway we started going downhill toward Boston Harbor. I had seen the house only a couple times, but I recognized it—tall and narrow, almost on top of the houses on either side, cave-like two-car garage on the ground level. The driver pulled into a spot in front of it. There are those stairs Mom said she hated, I thought. Nana and Papa shouldn't be climbing up and down that steep flight every day.

I dragged my suitcase up the outside flight of stairs, each step just a little harder than the one before it. When I got to the outside entry to Papa and Nana's flat I rang. Papa yelled, "Judy, go unlock the door, will ya?"

Mom came down the narrow inside stairway. As I painfully lugged my suitcase up the stairs, she said, "How they do this all the time I'll never know. I had forgotten what a pain in the ass it is."

"You're So Beautiful," 2004

Mom showed me her old bedroom. "It's amazing to see it now. They haven't changed anything in thirty-five years!" she exclaimed. The small room was papered in a flowered pattern on a dark blue background. The furniture was blonde wood in that "American modern" style of fifty years or so ago. One of the pieces was a sit-down dresser with a low counter and a round mirror in the middle flanked on each side by higher counters. Mom sat on the bed. "And this is the same lousy mattress."

Nana showed me the little room with double shuttered doors off the living room. "Here's your room," she said. It was small but comfortable. I had a view of the street below and the empty lot across from the house, and if I peered through the buildings in front of me I could glimpse at Boston Harbor a little below the elevation of the street the house was on. Across the street and to my right was Seaport, a restaurant and pub in what I assume was typical South Boston style. This isn't half bad, I thought.

I could already see that Nana and Papa needed to do some serious updating and repairs to the place. That was unlikely to happen, I knew. Papa's attitude was always, "It's good enough!" The appliances were probably fifty years old, but they worked. The bathtub's inside finish was dulled from the repeated use of cleanser and it had a hand shower that barely worked. The carpet was almost worn down to the nap and the linoleum in the kitchen and bathroom was cracking and starting to come up. Still, I could see the location was terrific, within walking distance of Carson Beach and with a variety of bars, pubs, restaurants, and stores on nearby Broadway. I wonder why these houses aren't being snatched up and renovated, I thought. I found out soon that many of them were being purchased by young professionals and families who realized they could get a lot for the money in Southie, including the fact that it was also near a beach.

"Lisa, I don't even know if I'd know what Tommy looks like now." Mom was standing in the doorway. She continued, "But I feel he's so close by."

I suggested we all go to The Clam Box for lunch. "Okay, Papa?"

"Okay, Lisa, but first I need to pay a bill. You and Judy can come with us."

It wasn't a request, but an assumption. My grandparents have always paid their bills the old fashioned way, by first cashing their Social Security checks and then stopping in person at the utility companies to pay their bills. Oh boy, here we go, with Nana driving, I thought. We only had to get up to Broadway—not a bad walk for someone my age—but I offered to drive.

"I need to go to the bank to cash the checks," Nana said. "I'll meet you out here in a minute."

Papa, Mom, and I walked a short distance by the Radio Shack, a deli, a Walgreen's, and a barbershop. Papa said, "This is where I've gotten my hair cut the past fifty years." The shop was a narrow storefront.

I said jokingly, "Papa, I need a haircut."

Guess I shouldn't joke with Papa about haircuts! He took my arm and said, "Come on in here, they'll cut your hair."

"Papa, I can't get my hair cut there!" He didn't hear me—or maybe he wasn't listening.

"Come on. I want to introduce you to Octavio." So in we went, my mother, my grandfather, and I. The narrow shop was like an old movie set: old tile on the floor, the paneled wall dotted with faded newspaper clippings about the Red Sox and Celtics, some framed and some just taped up, along with a map of Italy and an article about "Octavio's Barber Shop" in a black frame. The well-used barber's chairs looked like they were covered in leather, not just Naugahyde. Turquoise plastic chairs for customers sat against the paneling.

A barber I guessed was Octavio was in the process of cutting a man's hair. The man's hair was already short, sort of a longish butch. He had a nose that looked as if it had been broken several times and there was a cut on his ruddy cheek. They both smiled at me. I smiled back—not many other choices when you're looking at a guy who might decide to try to paste a smile on your face if you don't look friendly.

Hmmm. I had an idea. "Papa, you go on and pay your bills and I'll ask Octavio to cut my hair." My mother and grandfather left to pay bills and find Nana, and I sat down in the cracked vinyl barber chair. He said, "So, Hon, where you from?" He had an Italian accent.

"Well, I live in Alabama with my family, but I'm originally from South Boston."

"Southie? Why did you move away from Southie?"

I took a breath. I mentioned the Boston Irish group and how we had run away from my father. "I don't know all the details, but we moved away when I was four years old. Do you happen to know my father? His name is Tommy Connor."

A short pause, but still a pause. The barber looked down at "Bruiser" in the chair. Bruiser looked up at him. And then they both looked at me.

"Of course we know your father," the barber said.

"Look, I'm only here for a couple days. My family is terrified—terrified—of my father. Here's my business card with my cell on it. Will you get it to my father? But whatever happens, please don't let any of my family know."

The barber winked at me. "Okay, Hon. I'll see what I can do." By that time, my mother, grandfather, and grandmother were all walking in and we got in the car and headed on to the Clam Box.

* * * * *

As I was driving everyone back to the house about two hours later, my cell phone rang. Oh, shit! I thought—I almost said it. It was a 617 area code, a Boston area code. I don't know anybody else in that area code.

I dropped Papa off and drove Mom and Nana to the grocery store. "You guys go in and do your shopping," I told them. "I'll sit outside and check my messages."

So there I was, in South Boston, Massachusetts, listening to a message from my father. "Hon, Hon! This is the most beautiful day of my life! Thank you, thank you, thank you so much for contacting me. I can't wait to see you, I can't wait to see Timmy and Scotty. God bless you, God bless you, God bless you!"

I called the number back. "Oh, hi, Hon, this is Peter!" I thought, who is Peter? "This is your Uncle Peter. Your father's not here right now. I know he's real excited that he's gotten in touch with you and he can't wait to meet you. He'll call you right back."

We got back to the house and turned on a movie. All of a sudden my phone rang. Same phone number as before. "Oh, this is my friend Andrea," I announced, getting up.

I have to stop for a moment here. I was afraid when I saw that number again. I wasn't afraid for myself, but I was afraid of how my mom and grandparents would react if they found out I was looking for Tommy. No way could I tell them who was calling me. "I gotta talk to Andrea—she's just been on a cruise and she is dying to tell me about it," I said, and I went down the inside stairs to sit on the outside steps to be sure I was far enough from the possibility of my family hearing my conversation.

We made arrangements to meet the next night because he had a fishing trip planned with someone and he didn't think he could cancel it. That sounded early enough for me. I needed to prepare myself, though it was hard to keep quiet about it.

Early next morning he called me. I was already in my little room with the door closed. "I couldn't sleep last night and I cancelled my fishing trip. Can we meet?"

I hadn't slept, either. My mind was racing, wondering. What does he look like? What will he want to know about us? I had so many questions for him.

This was a perfect idea, because I loved going for a walk on Carson Beach in the morning. I could put on my Tigers baseball cap and Nikes without any questions being asked. "Okay. But understand, everybody is afraid of you. So . . ." We planned we would meet away from the house so the family wouldn't see him.

I passed Woody's L Street Bar, where some scenes of the film *Good Will Hunting* had been shot. I passed another little hole-in-the-wall that was even called "Good Will Hunting." What is this going to be like? I asked myself. I saw

Sketch of Me and Tommy by my friend Dr. Ronald S. McDowell,
Artist and Sculptor.

a man in a fresh white apron outside a small grocery store helping the driver of

a Great Eastern Seafood truck unload some boxes. A very old woman with a

scarf on her head and wearing a grey raincoat that must have been fifty years

old was using a walker to inch her way up Eighth Avenue. When Mom finds

out I wonder if she'll freak out, I thought.

There it is, the spot we said we'd meet. I saw a small man standing on the

sidewalk. I guess that's him, I told myself.

And then he walked toward me. He said three words. "You're so beautiful."

"I Forgive You," 2004

There in front of me stood Tommy Connors, alleged mobster and my father. And I said to him, "You're so tiny!" If he stood up straight he might have been about five feet five inches tall. I was at least four inches taller than he was. There must not have been an ounce of fat on him. He had curly grey hair, a little thin, brushed backwards off a high forehead. His face looked youthful, with a faintly rosy glow that made him the picture of good health. His brown Irish eyes sparkled with intelligence, shrewdness, and energy. He was wearing a shirt in a rather large pattern of peacock blue and teal, and he had a gold chain around his neck. Around his slim waist was a belt with a big silver buckle in the shape of a deep-sea fish of some kind.

He smiled at me and took my arm. "You wanna take a walk on the beach?" he asked. "Come on, Honey. You are so beautiful," he said again. When I raised my right hand he said, "I know that ring. I gave that to your mother."

Now wait a minute, I thought. My mother always told me that the ring came from my grandparents. But I didn't say anything to him about it.

So we walked along Carson Beach, people passing us or nodding "Hello" as they went by. I heard over and over, "Hi, Tommy". . . "Hey, Tommy. . ." When they were out of earshot my father would say something like, "He's so-and-so. His son died of AIDS," or "He has hepatitis." All of those locals apparently had a story to tell. He told me about Boston's needle programs and how he helped various organizations. He talked about the kids he was mentoring in the skill of boxing.

"You sound like Matt Damon or Mark Wahlberg but with the fast talk style of Danny DeVito," I said. His accent was just what I would have expected. He sounded like a stock character in an old gangster movie.

"No, Honey. They sound like me. They got the accent down pretty good, though. Matt and Mark are both from around here." I smiled at the way he said "heah" for "here." I recognized right away that he had personality plus.

We were walking, walking, walking. . . .Thoughts were impossible to even express. We made plans for lunch and after a bit I went back to spend the rest of the day with my grandparents, knowing they had some things they wanted me to help them with.

When I got back to Nana's and Papa's, my mother and her old girlfriend Bridgett, who had helped us escape from South Boston in the disguised utility truck so many years ago, were about to head out the door to spend some time together and then go to lunch. They tried to talk me into going with them, but I said, "No, I've got to exercise. I've been gaining weight and I don't feel good. The best way to feel better is to exercise."

"Okay, Lisa. I keep having these feelings about Tommy. I don't even know what he looks like but it feels like he is so close by." Mom repeated the same thing she had already said several times before.

"Let's go, then, Judy," said Bridgett. I walked down the two flights of stairs with them. "Bye, Mom, bye, Bridgett. See ya in a little while."

I went down the street in the opposite direction from the way they were headed, toward D Street, to meet Tommy for lunch. Seeing me, he got out of his car. "God bless you, Honey, you're so beautiful," he said, and he handed me an envelope. "I missed out on a lot of birthdays with youse. It's just a little something, Honey." I didn't make a move to look inside it and he didn't seem to expect me to, so I stuck the envelope in my back pocket, saying "Thank you," and he drove us to a fancy restaurant that he insisted on taking me to.

I was more nervous than I had thought I would be. I chugged beers—I mean I really chugged beers. "Scotty really wanted to meet you," I said. I described Scotty's long battle with mental illness and his funeral. "Mom is very afraid of you. She's never gotten over her fear of you. She even told my grandparents a couple of years ago that when they died she would not come to their funerals because she was afraid to come back to South Boston." I told him about how my mother always looked over her shoulder before she got into a car and how when she got out of a car she looked all around her. I told him that even with the distance and many years between them, she still lived in fear he'd send someone out after her.

I cried a little. My father cried, and he cried and he cried and he cried. "Honey, I'm so, so, so, so sorry," he said. "I wish I could have been there for Scotty." He wiped his eyes on the white cloth napkin in his lap. I had never seen a man cry so deeply and I knew his tears were sincere.

A couple of times he told me he always worried about me. "Men are ruthless," he said. I knew what he was trying to find out but I didn't say anything. "Boys can take care of themselves, but girls, they need someone to protect them." I knew he wanted to be reassured that I had never been molested because that was his biggest fear for me.

After our orders came, I kept looking at the door. I had a strange feeling, like my mother was going to walk in any second. "I'm not usually like this,"

I thought, but I kept looking toward the door, watching the door. And she didn't come in. But I still had a feeling that she was close by.

When lunch was over, my father took me back and dropped me off near, but not right in front of, the house. I stumbled up the steps. All that beer was getting to me. "Gotta lie down," I thought. The couch looked good.

Just before I lay down I took the envelope out of my pocket. It was a stack of fifties and they looked like they hadn't been in circulation in years. I held them up to the light. I knew how to look for serial numbers on bills because of my years of waitressing. I had been stiffed once and I learned my lesson after that. Where did these bills come from? Where did he get them? Had they been buried somewhere? I wondered. My spinning head got the better of me and I passed out on the couch.

* * * * *

"Bridge, that seafood platter was good. I'm glad we went there." My mom's voice woke me up a little.

My mom and her old friend were talking about the restaurant where they had eaten. "So, Mom, where did you go?" I asked thickly. I yawned.

It was the same restaurant where my dad and I had eaten. We must have passed within five to ten minutes of each other. I kept that realization to myself, though.

My mother said, "There's something so strange about this visit." She got up and went into the kitchen.

I said softly, "Bridgett, Bridgett, I have to tell you something. I met my father for the first time today and I've been with him twice today. I'm gonna tell my mother but I don't know . . . do I tell her now or do I wait until she's back in Oklahoma? She's so afraid."

Bridgett said, "Ya gotta tell her now." So my mother came back in and I said, "Sit down." And it was like she knew. I said, "Mom, I met my father today."

She said, "I knew it! I knew you were up to something! Weren't we talking about it, Bridgett? I knew it!"

I said, "Mom, I wanna share some things with you. My father shared his confession about his life, about things that I don't even remember, bad things. I shared with him about Scotty and I told him about your fear, about your level of fear all these years. He cried and he cried and he cried. Mom, I truly believe it would help you overcome your fears if you would just meet him."

She said to me simply, "Okay." I couldn't believe it but I certainly wasn't going to let this opportunity pass by. I called him immediately and he said he'd be outside the house in twenty minutes.

Meanwhile, my grandparents walked in. And Mom said, "Lisa met Tommy."

Papa said, "Huh! What the hell are you talking about?" He sounded totally dumbfounded. It didn't seem to register who "Tommy" even was.

When Mom told her she was about to meet with my father, too, Nana looked both frightened and confused. "What are you doing? How long you gonna be gone? I don't understand!"

We met him outside. He hugged my mother, which was a surprise even to me. He then guided her to the front seat and I sat in the back.

And off we went. I wondered what my mom was thinking. We didn't know where we were going, and yet we had agreed to get in the car with a man my mother had been sure at one time had had a hit out on her. I wasn't afraid, but I wondered if she was.

Tommy told Judy, "I live with Peter now." I had met my Uncle Peter earlier that day, too.

My mother said, "I'd like to see Peter."

"Okay," answered Tommy. So we pulled up a narrow little street and stopped at a narrow three story house with shingle siding painted red. It had white trim and a red door. The basement level was half above ground. It was constructed of grey concrete and had frosted glass block windows. There was no yard in the front.

"Come on in," Tommy said. "Let me go get Peter."

We sat in the living room as Peter came down from upstairs. "Judy, you look good," Peter said. He went over to kiss her on the cheek. "Youse all want a beer?" he asked.

"Sure," I answered. Just what I need, another one, I thought. Oh well, how often do you not only get to meet a father you barely know but also get to see your mom talking to a man she had been deathly afraid for most of your life— and all on the same day?

"Yeah, I'll take one," my mom said. I was flabbergasted. She never drank beer. She downed it quickly and when Peter asked her if she wanted another one, she answered right away, "Yeah." I had never seen her do anything like that. Every part of her body was shaking, her arms, legs, every part. I didn't know whether to go over and hug her or to slap her and say, "Get a grip!"

My father spoke up. "For the love o' me, Christ, for the love o' me, twenty-

My father and me six months after we met.

seven years, Judy, still livin' in fear! For the love o' me!"

She said, "Tommy, don't you think I have reason to be fearful o' you?"

He looked over at her. There was a pause and then he replied, "Well, I guess you have a point. But not for twenty-seven years! Judy, I always knew that you were a good person with a good heart. I always knew that you were a good mother. I always knew that you would raise the children with love. And that's what gave me peace, Judy. And I'm so sorry. All of those years, all of the fear, everything I've put you through. And I'm sorry that I wasn't there to support you through Scotty's illness. I'm so, so sorry for everything."

My mother, the former Judy Connors, looked at her ex-husband, Tommy Connors, for about a minute. Then she said, "I forgive you."

Another three words. Three words. They ended almost three decades of being afraid.

MY SOUTHIE FATHER

Mom and I left Nana and Papa's together, sharing the expense of the cab to the airport. She had to catch a plane to Tulsa, and as we quickly hugged good-bye, she said, "I'll think about going to live with Nana and Papa." I couldn't believe it. She went to her gate, and I went to mine.

When I arrived to Atlanta, I picked up my car and drove back to Auburn. My dad had given me his cell number, telling me not to share it with anyone.

I talked to him fairly often during the next few months. He told me he wanted me to meet his girlfriend, Rita. "She's a wonderful person. I been with her now nine years," he said.

This was a busy time for my new business. PEPS was planning more and more AU events, and through those connections I was also finding myself more and more connected with prominent members of the city and university. Dale, workaholic that she was, would often get to the office as early as 6:00 a.m., and I'd have to nearly kick her out in the evenings. If I wasn't working on an event behind the scenes, I was a participant.

In 2005, around the time of year Scotty had passed away, my mom and I decided to take a trip to Boston again. We didn't say it to each other, but I knew she felt, as I did, that a trip there together would help deaden the painful memories. I also knew how deeply it had hurt my grandparents that they were unable to attend Scotty's funeral due to a Boston snowstorm causing the airport to close. Mom and I knew that having the four of us together on the anniversary of Scotty's death would be good for all of us. I asked Steve to join us but he wouldn't.

I had already planned to have dinner with my father and his girlfriend. When we got to Southie, I called my father and asked, "Would you mind if Mom comes?" He said that was fine with him.

We decided to go to the Seapoint, just down the block from my grandparents' house. While we waited for my father and Rita, I asked a guy in a South Boston firefighter's jacket sitting nearby, "Would you mind taking a picture of my mother and me?"

He agreed, snapping a picture with a disposable camera Mom had brought. Then he asked, "So what's your name?" followed quickly by, "Can I buy you a beer?"

I thought, why not? It's harmless. The guy's just being friendly. He bought both my mom and me a Coors Light and we talked a little, just small talk, nothing personal. We talked, that is, until my father and Rita came in. "Excuse me a minute," my father said. My father took that young firefighter over to the bar and the man came back and said good-bye to my mother and me.

Mom had never met Rita, but Rita is the kind of person you warm up to immediately. She was (and is) a short, pretty brunette with an endearing Boston accent and a friendly, easy-to-talk-to manner. She and Mom were chatting pleasantly.

"Hey. What kinda beer ya drinkin'?" My father sat down. Somehow he had become Tommy Connors, Southie tough guy. His accent was even more pronounced than it had been earlier that day. I could hear laughter coming from the bar, but I couldn't see the man we had been talking to.

"What happened to that firefighter guy?" I asked.

"Nothin', Honey."

"You're lying!" Mom said abruptly.

Rita looked at my father and then looked at my mother as if she was trying to interpret what was underneath their short words to each other. I said, "I'm going to find out and it's better for you to tell me." My dad said nothing. "Okay then. In fact, I'm going to ask him to dance." All three of them looked up at me as I spotted him and walked over.

To make a long story short, he wouldn't have anything to do with me. "Can't right now, Lisa," he said.

"So what happened?" I asked him.

"Well," he said, "Your father got in my face and said, 'Do you know who I am?' And I answered, 'Yes, Sir, I do.'"

I can imagine that exchange—Tommy, all five feet five of him, looking the guy in the eye and warning him, "That's my daughter and my ex-wife and I want you to stay away."

So the guy got his beer and left. My father didn't tell me anything. But my mother knew. She knew. She knew Tommy Connors.

And yet she could laugh at him. What a small miracle.

Every time I watch a movie like *The Godfather* I think of my father. That fireman knew exactly who my father was. Even though my father was sixty years old. Even though he was "retired," as he would tell anyone who asked him about his past. He may be retired, but he had a reputation, and I could easily see he still worked to keep it alive.

An old friend of my father's, Fran Hurley, recently characterized my father as "a pit bull in a fight." He commented, "He can size up a person in an instant. He'll hang on until he wins. You do not want to get into it with him."

He walks around with his back straight and chest out and stands with his arms crossed, exuding a "don't mess with me" attitude. He knows everybody in the Southie community, it seems, and has no shyness about talking to anyone or telling them what's what. He can seem a little overpowering and bossy if you don't have a sense of humor about the advice he gives on anything from the color of your hair to your weight. Every time he talks to me, he warns me about watching my health. Last time I visited Southie he said to me, "Now, Honey, you need to take care of that butt of yours. Eat your Raisin Bran in the morning and exercise at least five days a week."

Yet he treats Rita with love and an easygoing respect, and she obviously loves him, too. He's a great conversationalist, very entertaining, and very generous.

That's my Southie father. That's the man my mother was terrified of for twenty-seven years. That's Tommy Connors.

My father and me on Papa's 90th birthday.

"I Think You Should Write It"

"But I didn't even finish high school! I couldn't get in college!" The man talking to Steve had a mouthful of gold teeth and at least two gold chains hanging around his neck. We were at Touchdowns, a local hangout that I had dragged Steve to. He didn't enjoy being "Lisa's husband" at social places, but I noticed he often found someone to talk with and afterwards would tell me about the interesting conversations he had had.

As I mingled nearby with a bank president acquaintance and some other local business people I heard the man say, "You have your Ph.D. You're a professor. I bet you've had a nice quiet life. I've been involved in some bad things."

And Steve said, "Lemme me tell you about my wife. . . ." That's all I heard because an older lady I knew tapped me on the shoulder.

Later, while driving home, Steve said to me, "You know all those years you said to me you had this idea to write a story, to write a book? I believe you should write it."

He told me that the man had been interested in how I managed to graduate and how I had gone on to be the owner of a successful business. Well, maybe I should write a book, I thought.

I had overcome some obstacles and found my father and he had told me details of his life. For the first time, I realized he was a person, not just a one-dimensional stand-up figure. I realized he had a story, too, and our stories intertwined in some curious ways. I wondered if I could combine some of his story with mine.

I knew I wasn't ready, though. I was gun shy about baring my life to the world because, before meeting my father, I had told very few people about my past. Even when I had revealed parts of my history, I had left out the details related to my father. And when I had shared some of my story, the result was not always good. I remember one painful episode involving some neighbors in Auburn.

They were parents to two boys about the same ages as Zack and Trey. We moved into our house near theirs in January, and by August we had become good friends with them. They sent me balloons on my birthday and we did nice things for them, too. Our children played together jumping on the trampoline and riding bikes. We went out to dinner with them and sat on the patio together from time to time sharing a beer or two.

They were a lovely family. I saw them as probably the most Christian family I had ever been close to, very involved in their church. However, their Christian charity wore thin after they learned the truth about my past. One evening when we were drinking margaritas together as our kids played outside, I started sharing some of my background. I told them about Scotty, my teenage pregnancies, my lack of education, and so on. They seemed very interested and asked me a lot of questions.

But something changed between our two families after that evening. They stopped answering their phone when I called and or did not return calls when I left messages on their answering machine. My boys, missing their playmates, would run over and knock on their door, but they wouldn't answer it. If they did answer the door, they'd tell my children their children couldn't play. Not long after the friendship between our families cooled, our neighbors moved. I wondered since then if they moved to get away from us. I never knew.

I had been burned and I didn't want it to happen again. As I thought about putting my past on display, I remembered how rejected I had felt. I was well aware of one of my greatest weaknesses: I wanted too much to be liked. I took it very hard when I thought someone didn't like me, whatever the reason.

Oh well. "Put it behind you," I told myself, and I did for the most part. But I still wasn't ready to take the risk of once again finding out I was being judged for some events and circumstances in the past that I had overcome, even if my story might be helpful to someone else.

Besides, there were some issues between Steve and me that needed fixing if there was any chance to do that. He had recently told me, "Lisa, I just can't compete with you. You are the perfect mother, the perfect business person, the perfect everything." He went on to comment on my business ethics and how I tried to help others sometimes to my own detriment, ending with the haunting words, "I can't compete."

For the life in me I couldn't understand why Steve felt he had to compete with me. If anything he was the one with three college degrees, he was the one with "Ph.D." behind his name and who was often referred to as "Dr." Steve. We tried counseling in an effort to save our marriage, but the sessions only brought things simmering in the pot to a boil. It had been nearly three years since my father came into my life and I wished Steve had met him. I wished he would go back to Southie with me to spend time with my grandparents. My trips back to Southie had been solo for several years. "It would be so meaningful to me if you would go with me to Boston to meet my father and to see my grandparents. My grandparents are not much longer for this world," I pleaded.

My next visit to Southie, just after we had discussed in counseling his refusal to come to Southie with me, was a rough time. I walked Carson Beach observing the happy couples hand in hand, a few making out on the beach. The marriage counselor was shocked during our next meeting to learn that my visit had ended up being solo again, even after we had talked about just that in the previous meeting. That was our last meeting with the counselor. Our marriage was over. We both knew it.

Steve was, and is, a good man. It seemed as though all the reasons Steve fell in love with me became the same reasons he fell out of love or became threatened by me. I did know he was becoming an angry man. That anger sometimes came out verbally, not just towards me but also towards Zack. The other details of the ending of our marriage are going to remain between us out of respect for Steve, as well as for Zack and Trey. There was responsibility on both sides, and I think he'd agree with that assessment.

There were some financial details to work out between us. Prior to our divorce we had taken equity out of our house to put some money down on a two-story storefront in downtown Opelika as a location for PEPS. Opelika, east of Auburn, was on the front-end of a revival and I wanted to take advantage of it from the beginning. I could see it. I loved the concept of being part of something from its inception and then it becoming a reality. This concept is true in regards to planning an event, too. The city has a number of sites on the National Register of Historic Places and its downtown is quaint and charming, with great potential. I thought to myself, everything is possible; we just have to believe in it. Adjacent to downtown are many restored nineteenth century and turn-of-the-twentieth century homes, and the majestic Lee County Courthouse sits just across the back of the building.

The building itself was a little ramshackle but its basic structure was sound and it was in a near-perfect location with a large parking lot behind it. For me, the cherry on top of the sundae was an impressive view out back of a historic downtown church and the Lee County Courthouse with its red brick exterior, its white columns, and its historic clock tower rising above the city. What sold me most about the building was its magnificent direct view of the courthouse and water fountain. I could envision a loft apartment or social gathering area upstairs with a balcony that would allow people to enjoy that view, which was lovely by day and charmingly romantic at night. On the ground floor there was enough square footage to carve out some small offices to rent to tenants, thus defraying the monthly mortgage payment on the building, and there was plenty of room for two nice offices for Dale and me, a large conference room, and a kitchen and restroom. The front area allowed for a pleasant reception and waiting area.

As part of our divorce settlement I agreed to reimburse Steve for half of that down payment made from our joint equity in the lake property. When the divorce was final, I began renovating the building, and as soon as the loft apartment was livable, Zack, Trey, and I moved in and I put our Auburn house up for sale. Then I changed my mind about selling. I ended up renting out the house with an option to buy to someone I wanted to help, a single mother of two young children.

Steve commented to me after the divorce that "it was fair, could have been better, could have been worse, but it was fair." The loft apartment was everything I could have hoped for and more. It reminded me of Oklahoma combined with a bit of a "Southie" feel. It was mine and I was proud of the accomplishment, especially considering how difficult it was to close the loan for myself. Getting creative with the financing and partnering with both a bank and with a government entity wasn't easy and took time, but I finally closed the deal. We took the salvaged wood from the downstairs ceiling and placed it on the old floorboards and refinished it, and we uncovered the original exposed brick walls so that the brick could be seen again. We designed the kitchen to include a large square granite island that can seat ten or more people while still allowing for great flow and chances to mingle. I planned the loft from the beginning as a versatile place to use for cocktail parties and small meetings or events if we moved out of it. And the view— my little table and chairs on the balcony became a relaxing place to kick back and put my super-charged day to rest which I needed.

The adjustment to being innocent parties to divorce wasn't easy. We went through some rough times in the months after the divorce was final, with neither Zack nor me sleeping much. As with the details of what went wrong with Steve and me, the details will remain within our family. But I know the decisions made in the end were the right decisions not only for me but also for the boys, especially for Zack.

Zack and Trey know Steve still loves them. They have handled the breakup with resiliency. I hope they think that's what counts. Maybe they inherited their ability to adapt from me and from my father, since he is the one who gave it to me. I hope so. If I had a list of character traits I could pass on to my children, resiliency would be one of the top items to leave to them, along with a good work ethic, a survivor mentality, and a heart to make the world a better place in which to live.

PASSING THE HUG

I have to admit it: I was lonely. Yet my business was going well and I didn't think much during the week about how empty I felt. On weekends, though, I felt the loneliness hanging around the loft like the Ghost of Marriage Past. Zack and Trey were occupied with their many friends and Zack had a girlfriend. I hoped I might find some comfort or friendship at a church. Steve wasn't a churchgoer and since moving to Auburn I hadn't gone to church, but newly single, I must have visited nearly every church in Auburn and Opelika. However, choosing the first church to attend was not an easy choice.

In my mind's eye I saw myself at the age of nine or ten as I was passing an African American church near the Southside community in Tulsa. I'd walk by it on Sunday morning on my way to the QuikTrip to pick up a newspaper for Guy and I'd hear loud, enthusiastic singing and clapping. Someone would play long glissandos on the piano and the building would almost shake when a man's rich, deep voice shouted, "Hallelujah!" and the members of the congregation answered him with, "Praise Jesus!" Sometimes I'd sit down on a corner bus bench and pretend to be looking at the *Tulsa World* as the service let out. The people would hug each other, the men slapping each other on the back. They looked like they really loved each other.

That was the kind of church I wanted. I knew Reverend Johnny Green of a nearby predominantly African American church known as White Street Baptist and I decided to visit there. I wanted to know if I could feel the music deep in my soul like you might envision when watching a movie with an African American Baptist church choir. I wasn't exactly the usual Sunday morning visitor, but as I walked up I was greeted, and I was greeted and greeted and greeted. I sat down and was greeted some more.

A little bit later we "passed the hug." That means that people from all over the church hug each other. After that, all the visitors stood up and said what church they were affiliated with. When it was my turn, I told the truth: "My name is Lisa Ditchkoff and I haven't been to church other than weddings and funerals over the past several years."

At the end of the service the pastor invited whoever wanted an extra prayer to come forward. I did, and all of us held hands. It was like everything the pastor was saying was about me. I was crying so hard the tears were falling off my face and my nose stopped up. I wanted to rub it but I couldn't because I was holding hands!

After the prayer time the man next to me squeezed my hand and said calmly, "Everything's gonna be all right."

As I walked out, many people said, "Thank you for visiting. God bless you. Thank you for coming." I went to my car with tears in my eyes as I thought of the simple comforting words of the man holding my hand.

The joy those beautiful people passed to me on that visit remained in my heart during the months after the divorce. It developed into a litmus test by which I could judge the man I was talking to. The reaction from most of them if I asked them to go to that church with me was, "Uh, no, I don't think so" or just "No, thanks." They were history. A couple of the men didn't even call me back after that conversation.

Another church I attended was a large, well-established church of a mainstream denomination. I later had an opportunity to tell the pastor how I had felt when walking into his church by myself and this is what I said:

> *I walked up to the door and I wasn't greeted. And I walked in and sat down and I wasn't greeted. And there were people to the right of me and nobody came and sat on the left of me, and there were people up in front of me. And no one talked to me. I thought, "I feel invisible. Do they not see me?" Now your sermon was wonderful. But what got me was something that happened several times the following weeks after. Several couples and individuals I knew came up to me and said, 'Oh, I saw you at my church!'" If they did, why didn't they come over and greet me? I'm sure many people there knew I was going through a divorce since we live in such a small community. If they had thought about it, they would have realized I was hurting. Wouldn't you think that at least one person would have greeted me?*

I wish I could say that the experience I described was the exception, but it wasn't. I kept hoping I'd find a different, more welcoming, more caring spirit. I needed it. In the Bible Belt, where in some towns gigantic churches of four different denominations sit on the corners of an intersection, not to mention the Catholic parish just down the street, there didn't seem to be a wealth of Christian love.

LIFE'S MIRACLES

"There would be wiffle balls and plastic bats....The surfaces would be concrete so people in wheelchairs could move around." Danielle Tadych was the name of the tiny thirteen-year-old girl who had shared her dream of a creating a baseball field especially designed and outfitted for people with special needs and challenges.

The Make a Wish Foundation had chosen Danielle as one of its wish fulfillment recipients. "I'm sorry, Miss Tadych, but we don't buy land," they had told her. They did give her an option, though. She and her family could go to Disney World. Instead, she wanted to meet the President of the United States. The waiting list to meet the president was two years long, but still she chose to go to Washington, D.C., to the place where the leaders of our great country might be able to help her make it come true. When she and her traveling companions got there, hoping to find someone who could make things happen, the responses were very discouraging.

Most people would have given up. But not Danielle Tadych. She decided to share her dream with local clubs and organizations. The Lions Club took her vision and ran with it. At the time I met her, Danielle weighed all of maybe thirty pounds. I had learned she would never get any bigger than she was. She has a disability called *osteogenesis imperfecta,* which means her bones are fragile and subject to breaking without warning. She's had numerous surgeries to repair breaks of one bone or another, and her parents have had to retrofit a bedroom with a miniature toilet, sink, and bedroom furniture for her. She has to be carried or transported in a small wheelchair. Such challenges she has, and yet she is cheerful, bright, articulate, and full of faith. And so are her parents, whose opti-

Me, Hope and Danielle Tadych following Danielle giving her first public presentation to my Rotary Club of Auburn.

mism never fails to amaze me. I couldn't help thinking about how often I started my days by going into my boys' bedrooms just watching them as they slept, knowing the many blessings I have. Every morning watching them as they slept. Every morning I knew just how blessed I have been. I knew what it meant to love your child and I wanted to help Danielle's parents give their child her dream.

As I was mulling over my future, Danielle's dream was coming true. My heart got involved and I helped raise the funds for the planning and construction of the Billy Hitchcock Miracle Field Complex named after William Clyde Hitchcock, "Mr. Billy," a beloved former Auburn University athlete who later managed the Atlanta Braves and then moved to Auburn when he retired. He had recently passed away after a long and honorable life.

Mr. Billy was bedridden by the time I met him, but even though his body was shutting down, his mind was sharp. I often visited with him and showed him photos of Danielle, describing her dream of having a special place for children with disabilities to play baseball. After he looked at several pictures of Danielle, he held my hand and said, "Tell me more, tell me more." Sadly, he passed away before Danielle's dream could be realized, but we decided to honor his legacy by naming the Miracle Field after him.

As funding coordinator, I had the privilege of working with Danielle to see her dream become reality. Knowing her has made me wonder if there really are angels in disguise among us. If there are, she's one of them.

The fundraising for the complex lagged on and on, much longer than I would have imagined. Why was it so hard to raise this money? Why are disabilities so invisible? One problem is that there are too few places where people with disabilities can be equal participants. Danielle's dream wasn't just for herself to play baseball; her dream was to create opportunities for the whole community to come together. That's what the project was really about. After letter after letter, call after call, and people actually running from me when they saw me coming, finally the people of Opelika and Auburn came through. All it took was time and a little arm-twisting—and did I ever let that stop me?

During this time also I was approached by a couple of other organizations that needed a bit of help; however, one *really* needed help, as it was facing the closing of its doors. So off I went to help it. Today it is operating as a fine oiled machine, and I am still close to Danielle and her family. Next up, that story and other adventures in following my dreams.

ANOTHER DREAM

Learning to say "no" has always been a challenge for me. I've realized my gifts involve both projects and people, whether the job is taking something from an early stage and following it through to its completion, understanding the heart of an organization and helping through a knack for fundraising, or . . .

I set out to accomplish three specific dreams: creating a unique venue event center, completing my book, and establishing a nonprofit organization to service a tremendous gap in our community.

Here's how the third one came about: When I was helping my young friend Danielle with her dream of creating the environment for all the children who share her challenges as well as helping an organization to keep its doors open, I had a few encounters that have remained in my heart and ultimately have led to being a part of my long-term plans. A local businessman who is the father of a mentally challenged teenaged son started a conversation with me one day with the following words, "You know the story about my son's mother leaving us because of his challenges."

"Yes, I've heard," I replied.

"His daily challenges can be very difficult and even my wife (he had remarried) sometimes isn't able to handle him. What will happen to him when I'm gone? Nobody understands," he said. He lamented that there were no quality facilities for people with disabilities to live in our community, none even close to our community. He mentioned with sadness another couple who were considering taking their daughter with Down Syndrome to Kentucky to live.

Another local businessman knew I had a special place in my heart for people with disabilities. As he and I sat in his office one day, he said to me, "Let me tell you what my dream is. I believe there is a need for a local quality facility in which people with disabilities can live. I am not a rich man, but this is what I would be willing to do: I would be willing to purchase or have built a house, on the property, maintain it, and leave it to the organization in my will." Neither of these men knew that I was already aware of the need for a facility like this. When my family relocated to Auburn in 2001, I had looked for a facility such as this for Scotty. I hadn't been able to locate one.

These two men have a heart's desire that echoes my own. We know this need exists, and so I have decided to make the creation of this facility my third goal, both for the hearts of the children and for the parents. I've mulled over names of organizations and have finally made a decision to name it after a boy in our community whose father prays for the reality of it daily. If I have a gift, it is the ability to take a project from an early stage and follow it through to completion. I lie awake at night considering those who are in need of such a facility, locations, fundraisers, sustainability, every aspect of making this dream a reality.

Me on the front steps of the Coca-Cola building in the midst of the domino effect on business failures and difficulties that began due to the economic downturn.

THE YEAR OF THE DEPRESSION?

President George W. Bush addressed the nation on Sept 24, 2008 with one of the scariest speeches I've ever heard. Including a synopsis of the speech paints the picture of difficulties I begin to outline in this chapter and the following one.

Over the past few weeks, many Americans have felt anxiety about their finances and their future. . . We're in the midst of a serious financial crisis. . . As a result, our entire economy is in danger.

It would be easy to write off 2009 and the last couple months of 2008 as "The Year of the Depression," but I'd rather call it "The Year That Strengthened Me"—though I don't mean to imply that what followed that speech has been easy. It has been far from easy, but I can say without reservation that the tough times gave me the strength to forge onward with my dreams.

In late 2009, we lost Papa. Prior to his death, we had to put Nana in an assisted living home. While grieving these events, I was dragged into a lengthy lawsuit (as a witness), Trey dealt with some puzzling and potentially serious health issues, and Zack had to conquer some serious personal setbacks.

The timing couldn't have been worse for launching a new business. We faced many challenges in the process of seeing my long-time dream.

My dream had begun in 2003. By the time I remarried in 2008, I had already completed the renovation of the PEPS offices and the remodeling of the loft apartment where Zack, Trey, and I lived. Engaging an architect to draw up plans for a new building, I quickly realized the costs of starting from the ground up were too high.

That was okay, because my original vision had been to convert a warehouse. Then on March 25, 2008, I was driving the streets of Opelika inside the heart of the city and I passed a large warehouse for sale. I knew little about it other than it had been the home of the Coca Cola Bottling Company, which had closed its doors about two years prior. I scheduled an appointment to look at the property and the next day Dale and a handful of friends went in to see it.

As we walked into the first warehouse garage door, my heart started beating faster and chill bumps covered my body. I knew from that moment we had to have that building. But the building was much larger than what I had envisioned. We negotiated an extended due diligence period to evaluate the feasibility of the business as well as alleviate possible environmental concerns and evaluate the structural integrity of the property. We asked ourselves, do we purchase the property in this horrible economy? Can we get a construction loan with the amount of investment already in the purchase?

After multiple due diligence extensions right in the middle of the unforeseen, unexpected, and devastating national economy crash of 2008, we took nearly every penny we had available to us and purchased the property. When we had walked through those doors, there a dream was right in front of me, a dream to help build a community, a dream to be a resource for struggling nonprofits, for people, for businesses, and I was determined to make it a reality.

As I met with the mayor, economic development director, planning director, and other key city administrators, I realized how intrigued they were with the vision for building their struggling downtown Opelika. Yet we faced challenge after challenge. In 2008 and 2009 the roadblocks were not limited to multiple banks rejecting our request for a construction loan, but the reality that many banks were simply not lending at all. Altogether we had eight banks either reject our request for a construction loan and/or tell us they were frozen in their lending.

At the same time, my husband of several months had to tell me that he owed a substantial amount, close to $100,000, in taxes. He couldn't get a loan to refinance the house due to having *twenty-two* delinquencies on his credit report. I had perfect credit and a good banking history with this particular bank, and the refinance was granted with my signature.

Indeed, it was a difficult time. My late father-in-law was an absolute godsend, helping with generous infusions of badly needed funding. We considered selling cars, lake property, any or all of our investment properties, or depleting my retirement funds I had been saving since about the age of twenty-three. We were not even sure that these properties would sell but sold what we could. Our nation's economy was in such devastation and we were slap dab in the middle of it, facing the question of whether or not achieving this dream was even possible. Added difficulties were that the values of properties were continuously decreasing and loans were getting tougher for the average person to secure.

The situation felt discouraging, and there was much uncertainty as to where the money was going to come from. In spite of the uncertainty and as some funds freed up, we eventually hired a construction company to quote prices on demolishing or just completely gutting the property internally and engaged an architect to develop a full set of architectural drawings to include mechanical, electrical, and plumbing plans. Still, funding was desperately needed.

Finally, a bank president whom I've known for years, a man who would run when he saw me coming because he didn't have the heart to tell me "No" in regard to supporting the many community projects I had been involved with, took the time to at least consider the loan request. He asked questions and asked that we come back with research to help him understand better. Finally, the ninth bank request was approved after about a year, but only for a portion of the funding we requested. However, the list of contingencies was a bit lengthy, the primary of which was securing funding through SBA (Small Business Administration). To assure success, we secured an intermediary company to help with the process.

After weeks and weeks of research, Web surfing, phone calls to rental companies, unique venue facilities, and various lounges in larger cities, and road trips to Columbus and Birmingham to talk with owners asking for their help with estimated projections on expenses and income figures, we finally obtained all the information that SBA needed—the stack of information was the size of a hefty book by the time we were done.

Unfortunately, we were denied by SBA. So, we were back to the drawing board again, trying to ascertain additional information. Strange thing was, our contact with the first intermediary company wouldn't return calls. I believed she was discouraged, too. I must have left a dozen messages with her. We engaged a new intermediary company, one with a ninety-five percent success rate in securing SBA loans. Not long after we passed through their board, we submitted our application request to SBA.

Denied! Since SBA is headquartered in California and because the media announced that the state of California was facing bankruptcy at that time, I felt it was critical to create a picture of the more hopeful economic outlook of our quaint community as compared to California. Night after night after night, pulling fourteen to sixteen hours at a time, I researched and researched. I found every "kudos report," from the community being voted #1 for golfers in *Golf Digest*, to the news release about the influx of troops into Fort Benning, along with an abundance of other data and information that showed the attractiveness of the Opelika/Auburn community, and included it into the supplement report. Adding a detailed outline demonstrating the differences between how California SBA administrators may view economic conditions as compared to those in the Opelika/Auburn area, we were able to demonstrate a thriving community in many aspects despite the devastated condition of many other communities nationwide.

Had SBA denied us a third time, I had already decided the next step. I was going to fly to California, go to their headquarters in person, and not take another rejection as an answer. (And, if we had been denied by SBA for a fourth time, then I was going to fly to our nation's capital and perhaps get every media outlet involved right there in front of the White House.) I didn't have to. The third SBA request for a construction loan was approved in May 2009. It was a time of celebration.

Once we secured our funding, the City of Opelika agreed to support the business by eliminating building permit fees and sewage assessment fees, and it also agreed to alleviate some expenses to pave the property's parking lot providing a forty-thousand dollar grant. The support letter from the mayor was submitted along with the applications for loan considerations. Regardless of the state of the economy and what seemed to be continuous rejections, we pursued forward, never faltering in a vision and goal.

After receiving bids from several construction companies, we contracted with a small local company to start work in July 2009. Our previous construction calculations had resulted in inaccurate underestimates in regard to the remodeling of the 1938 building, so financial limitations forced us to reduce the scope of work and postpone some of the renovation we had initially hoped to do. However, we were able to make extensive improvements and to open doors and operate successfully. In addition to the approved construction loan, we have continued to create funding availability throughout the construction process and extend the scope of work.

To move forward in spite of these and other financial challenges, my focus became effective grassroots marketing. We hosted a neighborhood wine tasting, asking neighbors to rate the wines we were considering for our center. The distributors donated their product. I knocked on each door in our sixty-two-house neighborhood, talked with neighbors about the business, and invited them into our home. The event created a tremendous "buzz" which spread like a wildfire. While the area's largest newspaper outlet wouldn't do a feature story (but instead kept pushing us for advertising sales which we absolutely couldn't afford at that time), we became the feature of a small local one-year-old paper, front page and center, and had a small feature in another small newspaper that generated additional excitement over the business.

To further demonstrate support, the City of Opelika included the property surrounding the Event Center Downtown in their next phase to update the city streetscape with new paving, lighting, sidewalks, and landscaping. Additional city support has come from every department across the board within the city.

We had encountered some nearly equal but different challenges in securing a FF&E (Furniture, Fixtures and Equipment) loan. Regardless of the challenges, the excitement continued growing, in spite of the economic downturn and other factors that caused one of the city's largest employers, BF Goodrich, part of Michelin, to close its doors in 2009. Michelin Development continues to support the community by participating in local initiatives and providing local economic benefits; it is focused on contributing to the economic regeneration and long-term prosperity of the regions in which its sites are or have been located. The launch of Michelin Development provides an opportunity to have a far greater impact on Michelin's ability to support the regeneration of the local business community, and in particular, the creation of sustainable jobs. On January 14, 2010, our FF&E loan request was approved through Michelin Development.

We very carefully thought out every aspect of our business name, "Event Center Downtown." Having the word "Event" first in the name allows us to be found first in the white pages of a phone book, as well as in Internet searches. The word "Center" encompasses the long-range plans of the "one-stop shop." "Downtown" was added to boost the downtown economic development standpoint, thus helping other downtown businesses and the recruitment of new business.

Every time a fund-raiser is announced or a wedding reception is covered in the newspaper, or an invitation is received, people will have to think about "Historic Downtown Opelika," the heart of a city whose motto reads "Rich in Heritage with a Vision for the Future."

So, there we were, and still are—just a little dream but ultimately serving a larger purpose of helping build a community. Still, the aftermath of the 2008 economic downturn offers its challenges and sometimes it feels as if it is dragging on us.

Slowing the Bleed

"Are we going to sell the house?"

"Should we sell the car?"

These are only two of the questions we asked ourselves as we tried to survive the horrible economy. While our county tax rates had remained steady, our property values, like those of most people in the United States, had been continuously decreasing. Our rental properties were either vacant or rented out. One property was vacant for a year, so while it did not generate income, we still had a mortgage to pay.

Fortunately, my years of being a "tight wad" and knowing how to survive came into play. I was given the nickname of "Bulk Lady" at the area Kroger. Each Sunday, I would start the morning early, cutting coupons and making a list of what necessity items were on sale, at Kroger, CVS, Walgreens, Winn Dixie, and off I would go, making the rounds to each store. I even enjoyed it a little. I stopped purchasing extra kinds of things for myself, such as scented candles, higher-end shampoos, and so on. I used only the makeup at the bottom of my makeup bags. Because of my old or cheap makeup, I would carry a Q-tip in my pocket or purse and wipe the makeup from under my eyes throughout the day. We switched to Hamburger Helper or other meals costing less than fifteen dollars.

Everybody who has started a business is aware of the challenges in getting off the ground. The state of our nation's economy has contributed to some challenges that have been tougher than we would have thought when trying to start. Our six-month construction contract finally closed after thirteen months, complicated by battling a $68,000 materials lien on our property due to a subcontractor not paying for his materials. The concept of the conversion of an old Coca-Cola bottling plant into a state-of-the art event venue seemed like a large concept for a small community. We had to get people through the doors to see the vision even though construction was not complete. So, we hosted a "preview party" in the midst of the construction in April. The invitations were sent a week ahead and not only did those people attend but the word spread and people were even sneaking through the doors to see. The event was a huge success and the word traveled regarding the venue, which led to additional bookings.

Still, we were getting exhausted. We continued to work around the contractors, so cleanup in preparation for events was continuous and daunting. The expenses continued to grow: We had to hire an attorney to represent us, which meant more unexpected money out of our pocket. Once again we asked, "What do we sell?" Our properties were still either empty or rented at slashed monthly rates.

The emotional effects of the nation's economy have left many feeling scared, vulnerable, and hopeless. Unfortunately, so many people were and still are suffering in our community, some much more than we were. They're suffering because they have lost jobs, they've foreclosed on their homes and businesses, many others are afraid of losing their jobs. Some are acting fearful that they won't get paid for their services, and some are acting in ways that contradict their typical behaviors. Attorneys, architects, contractors, and other businesses that have always had steady contracts and stable income are acting out of fear. For example, some contractors are underbidding jobs to get the job and then making up the difference in inflated change orders or by ordering lesser priced, lesser quality items, such as (in our case) tile.

Here's an example of a contractor trick that I've learned. Send the client over to pick out limited tile options, as in our case. We didn't like the tile selections, so I asked, "What price range is this tile?"

"Most of it is 99 cents and some is up to $1.50 per foot," the owner replied. Back to the architectural plans, which simply state "$7 per sq. ft. for materials and labor?

Hmmm. . . .

I call and schedule an appointment with the owner of a carpet and tile company to ask what the breakdown of $7 per sq. ft. materials vs. labor for tile would be. He says that we should be looking at tile that's in the $3-$4 range. So, $3-$4 dollars for materials and $3-$4 dollars for labor is what our cost breakdown should be. The way the contractor structured our plans, his profit margin would be astronomical, and we'd be left with inferior workmanship. It pays to ask questions and be wise.

During that time I also received a call from someone in the know. Our architect had submitted a change in our plumbing, going from the copper as stated in our plans to PVC. I asked a lot of questions. I learned that the copper is much higher quality in comparison. Why would our architect, who was working for us and not the contractor, be working on behalf of the contractor to help save him money? I had to confront our architect, and he retracted his request for change. I think he hated me, but frankly, I didn't care. What he did was wrong.

It seemed that at every end we were experiencing some sort of attack and selfish act. I recall a conversation I had with our architect several months prior to this situation. He had looked up at me and said, "You're my only paying client currently." Was the architect working on behalf of the contractor to help save the contractor money in an effort to try and secure more business? I didn't know. But what I did believe, and still do, is that people, including our architect and our contractor and many others, have acted out of fear, fear of not getting their next job or contract.

That realization makes me wonder, how deep is the fear across this country due to the state of the economy? Or is the human hard drive wired to take care of oneself and survive sometimes to the detriment of others instead of really showing brotherly concern? If these people behaved this way due to the economy, then money is their god, but I bet they pretend otherwise! I do believe that there is a domino effect out there that was and is long, difficult, and continuous, and we were slap dab in the middle of it. I wonder if some of our painful experiences wouldn't have happened if the economy wasn't as bad as it is. Would people have behaved the same way if they had not been fearful of what the future holds? Would our construction have been completed in a timely manner with fewer change orders?

We had hoped that with the construction woes in the past, our motto could be "Onward and Forward" and that we could begin to focus our energy on more positive aspects of the development of Event Center Downtown. That was not the case.

Another certified letter arrived in the mail. On October 13, 2010, we received notice from one of our contractor's subcontractors that they were claiming a lien for any portion of the price that was not timely paid. The amount the contractor failed to pay was not listed in the letter. I emailed the president of the HVAC company, who informed me of the details. This amount owed was $16,915 and the debt was more than 120 days old. Before, it was a subcontractor who had committed fraud. This time it was the contractor. Furthermore, we were not out of the woods yet in regard to our construction loan because the government bond hadn't sold yet, as it was scheduled to sell in November.

The construction loan that stretched from its original six-month contract to thirteen months, meaning it was seven months delinquent, finally closed the paperwork on August 27, 2010. Frankly, we couldn't have survived without the support of my late father-in-law who helped us pay our monthly home mortgage and even groceries. Following the final closing paperwork, I sat slumped in the chair at the bank president's office. He said to me, "Lisa, knowing everything that's happened and how hard it's been, would you do it over again?" My reply, you can never let a dream die.

Eventually, I ended up in the office of one of the best lawyers in the area. He helped through the final construction woes without feeling taken advantage of. While my attorney and I met in his office conference room for a few hours, I realized he was a real person experiencing real life challenges, as well. I listened to him talk about some of his own personal hurdles and he listened as I unloaded some of mine. I felt protected from a legal standpoint in regard to the business and the construction woes, but I also felt that someone was listening who truly cares about the spirit of humanity and ultimately me as a person, a mother, and so on. At the end of some of our calls, he often commented, "The counseling session is over" and we would both laugh, and we still do.

A couple of months prior to my second husband and I divorcing, I found myself sitting on the kitchen floor, crying. I begged my husband, "Please just help me understand why you lie to me about everything." With no explanation, he left me sitting there. Trey came out of his room, picked me up, and wrapped his arms around me, squeezing me very tight. Not long after, while Trey and I were driving to a soccer tournament a few hours from Auburn, he said, "Mom, I didn't want to tell you this but I have a huge hole in my cleat. I've been just dealing with it, but I'm afraid that my foot might come out while I'm playing in the tournament. Do you have some duct tape?" I knew my sons were trying to conserve and be as resourceful as possible, like me. When I arrived home the next day, I walked into another lie or perhaps betrayal. My mind was made up at that moment to divorce. I couldn't help to think about an experience with one of my best friends a couple years prior to this point. Chuck Hurston, a former Auburn University football player, grabbed a hold of both of my shoulders real tight shaking me and said, "Lisa, you've lost the Lisa sparkle, the shine that makes Lisa so special and you've got to get it back." I realized I couldn't be the best person I could be when I was in a relationship that was toxic for me.

When my second husband and I divorced in 2012, my attorney was there for me representing me through it. Again, I felt protected. I found myself emotionally and physically exhausted. For the first time in such a long time, I was struggling with building back some lost self confidence. It's time to take charge of my life and build myself back up. I start a new chapter in my life today: Looking Forward.

MY LIFE TODAY

Today, I'm operating my second business, Event Center Downtown, and am doing exactly what I enjoy, which is incorporating events to benefit the community and more. I always enjoy watching families and friends come together to celebrate for such happy occasions. Always, though, I want to do more to reach out to help the people in the community and surrounding area. Just recently, a few events have been held at the Event Center Downtown that changed the lives of some special people.

Event Center Downtown, Greater Peace Missionary Baptist Church, Pleasant Grove Missionary Baptist Church, and Omega Psi Phi, Fraternity Inc., Nu Lota Lota and Sigma Delta Chapters held an event called "Defining Courage." James Owens, or "Big O," was Auburn University's first African American football player. Reverend Owens spent his life serving the Lord, ministering to individuals and families. The fundraiser purpose was to raise the funds needed to renovate his bathroom to provide handicap accessibility. Before and after James underwent neck surgery, he relied on his wife, Gloria, both emotionally and physically. Their bathroom in their home simply did not accommodate James to help stability and balance. Following recovery from an additional spinal surgery, the hope is he will qualify to be eligible to be added to the heart transplant list.

People from nearby communities participated to help raise proceeds for James. After everything was said and done, the monetary goals were met, and remodeling of the bathroom began immediately. Planning this event was only a little gesture to help someone who means so much to me. James and Gloria are great friends and that's what friends do: help each other when they need it most.

Another successful event was a Supermarket of Veterans Benefits and Professional Services, composed of nearly fifty veteran organizations to serve the families of veterans in honor of "Military Spouse Appreciation Day." With more than nine thousand veterans in Lee County alone, there are so many in need of help, but they are simply unaware of the resources available.

At the event, numerous veterans, their spouses, and families showed up and utilized the different services offered. Attendance at the Event Center Downtown was included representatives from the Pentagon as well as many state service agencies. Members of the community also attended to thank those who have sacrificed so much for the wellbeing of their country. Patriotism did not end when this event was over. One of the most recent events held at the venue also radiated red, white, and blue.

A Mayor's Breakfast hosted Mallory Hagan, 2013 Miss America, as the guest of honor. She was welcomed home to Opelika, where she is a native. Not even crowds and a crown can keep her away from her tiny hometown. Miss Hagan has and will continue to make Opelika, AL proud.

It's amazing what can happen in a short period of time, and Event Center Downtown has proven that. The events held reached out to individuals in need as well as entire families. James Owens, the veterans of Lee and nearby counties, Miss America, and the citizens of Lee County are so appreciative of people willing to go the extra mile to help others.

Spending time with my sons and friends, growing Event Center Downtown, and wrapping up this book have kept me busy lately. I am also actively involved in several civic organizations, so I stay busy, but I talk to my father often. Every so often I bake cookies or other things and deliver them to friends and neighbors as a small gesture to let them know they are important to me. Reaching out to others makes me happy.

I so enjoy baking lots of cookies (and this time I filled cute frog cookie jars) and delivering them to friends and neighbors. When my sons were young, I would send them off to deliver cookies to neighbors.

I'll never forget Trey at the age of about eight looking up at me with the most desperate look and tone in his voice saying, "But, Mom, why do we always have to give all of the cookies away?"

I'm so glad my two sons now appreciate the trait of generosity.

TOMMY AND JUDY

"And so it goes, and so it goes. . ." The old Billy Joel song comes to mind as I think of my father and my mother today. They are not only speaking to each other now, but have actually become great friends. They laugh with the familiarity of old friends who share lots of history when they're together. Seeing how Tommy and Judy have put the past behind them makes me think that bygones can really be bygones if we are willing enough to let them go. But I also believe that my father's apologies and his constant "thank yous" to my mom have really helped her overcome those hard feelings.

Mom retired from her job and did something I would not have believed she would do seven years ago. She moved back to South Boston to help take care of Nana and Papa in 2008. They really needed her, though they wouldn't admit it. She needed to go but her fear of change was evident.

After talking, talking, talking with her about going for a couple of years, I picked up the phone and called her best friend and boss, Linda. "My mom's retiring and needs to get to Southie. I'm going to get her a plane ticket to leave three weeks from now. She's going to need some friends to help with her stuff."

Linda agreed. So while I was sitting in a local travel agency arranging my mom's flight, I called my mom and said, "I talked to Linda, bought you a plane ticket, and you leave in three weeks. Linda and your friends will help you with your things. The ticket is purchased and there's no turning back."

She said, "OK." Mom's friends helped and off she went. I realized I was a bit bossy but I also knew my mom needed a push. Enough was enough and it was time for her to make a change.

On one of my visits to Southie after my mom moved there, I got a good belly laugh out of something Nana did, or at least we think she did. I was only in Southie for three days and brought just one bra with me. I got up in the morning after my first night there and my bra was gone.

I do mean gone. Mom, a friend who was helping me collect material for this book, and I looked everywhere. We looked under the beds, in the garbage, in the bathroom, in the dirty clothes, and in the drawers. In Nana's lingerie drawer there must have been thirty or forty bras of every color and style we could imagine. There were also some items that were out of place, such as a winter hat that Mom said Nana had been complaining the year before she couldn't find. But my bra wasn't in there.

The only place we did not look was on Nana herself which we probably would have done if we had had the nerve. I borrowed a bra from my friend, who thought the whole situation was very amusing. We didn't find the bra before I had to leave. Who knows? Nana may have worn it for awhile. Much later, Mom did find it, buried on a closet shelf among Nana's things when she moved her into an assisted living home. Mom told me that during the time she was living there, Nana would come into her bedroom in the middle of the night and go through her things as if looking frantically for something. "Get back in bed!" Mom would order her, and she did. We never quite figured out what Nana was looking for.

Mom's accent was back to its Boston roots, and then in 2012 she moved down to Florida after the passing of both Papa and Nana. She's a bit heavier than she has been in the past—she quit smoking a couple years ago when she had her eye surgeries and that may be why—but I think it was more than that. I think she is still mourning the loss of Scotty. I think she struggled understanding why things had changed in her marriage with Dempsey.

When she had moved back to Southie, I think she knew she needed to be with Nana and Papa, yet she had been so afraid to face her biggest fears. I'm so relieved that my mom no longer has to live with the fears that paralyzed her in her daily life for nearly thirty years. Perhaps it is a miracle.

Mom, Tommy, and Rita came to Alabama—together—in July 2009 and again in April 2010. What adventures we had! On the first trip, they were greeted by a welcoming party of about twenty-five of our friends. We cooked up a traditional Southern barbecue including Brunswick stew, something they had never heard of.

Tommy couldn't get over the size of our neighborhood yards. He tried convincing me that we had plenty of land to build at least one other house on our property, which is just under an acre. Wonder what our subdivision neighbors would do if we took his advice! He had never before seen flowering trees such as our crepe myrtles, those late summer beauties in colors of white to pink to magenta that are so loved in the South. Tommy had never tried hush puppies, red velvet cake, or fish tacos, but they all went home fans of all of those wonderful delicacies.

Tommy's favorite experience was a fish fry at our friends Don and Sandra Wilder's home. One of my favorite stories about the Wilders is about when their oldest son David went off to college at Mississippi State on a partial scholarship. Don and Sandra scrimped every way they could to send money off to help David and were determined to make a trip to Mississippi to visit. They saved every penny they could for gas and an inexpensive motel. To eat while there, they boiled hot dogs in a coffee pot. They are some of my favorite people in part because they are genuine, kind, hardworking, loving, and understand the meaning of sacrifice. They epitomize the phrase "salt of the earth."

That evening with my family and the Wilders, we enjoyed "sanging" together, and boy, was my family in for a treat. We turned up the sound and sang to the country song recorded by David Alan Coe . . . "And I'll hang around as long as you will let me, and I never minded standing in the rain, no, and you don't have to call me darlin', darlin', you never even call me . . ." Good food, good entertainment with dancing, too, friends and family. At last, the family I had been searching for since we left Southie under the cover of night in a blizzard long ago.

* * * * *

The last time I was in Southie was January 2011 for my grandmother's funeral. The time before that was to visit my grandmother, and the time before that was for my grandfather's funeral in October 2009. Nana and Papa were married sixty-nine years when he passed. My father attended all of the services for both my grandparents: the visitation, funeral, the burial, and the reception. My brother Tim came from Illinois to be with the family. My mother, father, and Tim came February 2012 for a reunion at Event Center Downtown that featured Brandon Jenkins performing at our Winter

Brewfest. I'll never forget how Brandon stood with Scotty his last years of his life and was his one true friend.

My father came to visit May 2013 for Trey's graduation. It was exciting for him to be a part of observing Trey's smiling face as he walked across the stage and received his diploma. The visit was great and was the first time we've spent one-on-one time together since we met in 2004. He got to know his two grandsons better and even got his final tattoo of a huge bass fish across his back. Some of my best friends came over for a small party, which we all enjoyed.

Trey, Zack and my father at Trey's graduation May 2013.

Since I first began my story, another interesting topic of both national and personal interest to me was the capture of Whitey Bulger and his girlfriend Catherine Greig. I imagine there will be lots of stories and, perhaps, movies coming out about one of the FBI's most wanted criminals and perhaps those he had been connected to.

My father was recently featured on Anthony Bordain's *No Reservations* "Southie" episode in which Anthony referred to him as a "boxing legend" and showed the tape from his infamous record-holding knockout. He has also been featured recently, along with Peter Welch, at the gym for an upcoming episode series on boxing in Southie at Welch's Gym which is scheduled to air on the Discovery channel July 2013. There are other happenings in the works, too. He loves these opportunities to be his gregarious self.

My father is guarded when someone asks him about what he's been doing lately. I do know he's walking the straight and narrow. He says he's enjoying his "retirement," fishing, shooting his bow and arrow, and giving boxing lessons. He can't see Red Shea; if he did, Red would be violating parole and thrown back into prison.

Getting to know the other half of where I came from has been an experience I find hard to explain with words. My father recently told me he had counted the kids he grew up with and out of thirty or so, fifteen or sixteen were doing twenty to life in jail and twelve were missing. "People ask me, 'How could you survive all that mayhem?' And my answer is, 'I survived with boxing. And I didn't do drugs or drink, except for a couple of beers." The key word in my father's answer is "survived." Tommy Connors is a survivor, and I got that quality from him.

My father instills something in me nearly every conversation. "To maintain good health, you need to be strong physically, mentally, and financially, because at any time one or more than one can go wrong. If you maintain these three things, then you can handle struggling in one or more of these things."

My mother is so laid back it's unbelievable and my father is quite the opposite. I know now that I do have a lot of his personality along with my maternal grandmother's. As I've listened to him talk about his childhood, teenage, and young adult years, I have guessed that he was always high-energy and extroverted, with a survivor mentality and innate intelligence that could have taken him far beyond the boundaries of South Boston, had a caring teacher taken an interest in him. Within the confines of his small Southie world and his lack of education somehow he managed to live large, even though he didn't always live smart. His Southie friends and acquaintances have told me that Tommy is a very smart man in spite of his lack of formal education. So maybe I should say, instead, that he didn't always live *wisely*.

And neither did I, as I'm pretty sure this book has underscored. I did some things when I was still a teenager that I could have worn on my future like handcuffs, letting them hold me back from being set free from poverty and a lack of education. But that survivor instinct inherited from my father helped me unlock those cuffs and walk forward to opportunity and freedom.

I am aware that I am also high-energy, extroverted, and more than a little bossy, as Tommy is, at times. In my case, I didn't begin to know I was an extrovert until I had my first job at the age of sixteen. Today I recognize that I can talk to anyone just like my father can. Neither of us has ever met a stranger. We both have an ability to connect with all levels of people and treat them all with the same amount of respect. If you went out to a restaurant with Tommy Connors, you'd know exactly what I mean. As soon as the wait staff comes to our table he begins talking to them as if he knows them and he's their special friend.

EPILOGUE

Most people would let negative experiences define them, but I decided to write my own version of Lisa Ditchkoff. I was forced to be a survivor in this world yet despite every obstacle faced thus far; I refuse to be the victim.

Writing my story helped me realize that my success in coming out a winner over the many bad decks of cards that were dealt me has the potential to be inspirational to others. Whatever the personal struggle, many become emotionally and spiritually paralyzed at the thought of facing these challenges. I know this firsthand. I have watched my mother's fear paralyze her everyday actions. I've wondered if my mother might have gone on to train to become a nurse if she would have overcome her fears sooner. If so, her life as well as the lives of her children might have been drastically different.

I almost let my chipped teeth and being nicknamed "Chip" by my school-age peers keep me shy and insecure. Then I realize with a smile, they were so intent on making me feel bad about my teeth that they didn't focus in on my caterpillar eyebrows! And I have to mention my feet, which someone called the "ugliest" ever seen. While my peers walked barefoot at the pool or lake, I wore socks to hide them and never wore sandals until my early twenties during my Oklahoma State University years. Insecurities or embarrassment can stop a person in her tracks, and they almost did.

Even when I have known I was judged by others, whether in my teens and early twenties or even recently, I have continued believing in myself. I even look at my feet today and think to myself, these are pretty good looking feet. These feet of mine have traveled many miles of insecurity, survival, resiliency, and ultimately triumph. This life has taught me how important it is to smile, laugh, and rise above, no matter how difficult the situation.

What I do is continue striving, learning, and doing what I love to do: help others. I'm sure that some people are going to judge me by what they read in this book, and that's OK, because I believe this story can give someone else the inspiration to achieve whatever it is they dream about in spite of their past or present situation and in spite of the economic downturn. If it helps just one person that is worth more to me than all the dispersions the gossip-mongers might cast on me.

For the past couple of years, I had planned to title my book *Fearless*, but then I realized that title doesn't accurately describe me because I am afraid like so many others of what the future holds, especially in regard to this country's economy. In spite of the fears, I have also decided to not allow my past pains and current fears to detour me from pursuing the things I believe are possible.

I was afraid to share some of my past, such as the abuse I've endured and mistakes I have made because of embarrassment of being judged. I especially didn't tell anyone that I was in hiding from the mob as that would have added more fuel to their fire. I've come a long way and have much to be proud of, including two awesome young adult sons who are now twenty-three and nineteen years old. Am I a proud mom? You bet. And I think I'm tough enough, and they're resilient enough, to tell this crazy life story of mine.

I believe there is a purpose in everything. Sometimes we don't understand why at the time, but I do believe that there is some great purpose in having overcome extraordinary obstacles, experiencing unbelievable pain,

My sons and me on my 39th birthday just after they cooked me dinner.

coming to know the hearts of these former Auburn University football players that I worked with for more than eight years, and finding my father, Tommy.

In spite of the bad decisions and the sometimes foolish or naïve actions both Tommy Connors and I have made in our lives, we have both led an uncommon life. I look toward the future with optimism, believing that what I put into my life is what I will receive from it. I am headstrong—even stubborn—for a reason.

I think it is important, especially more so today, to tell my story because I believe so many have given up hope, and hope is what builds a country. Hope is something that I will never stop believing in. Hope to provide inspiration is my purpose for sharing my story.

Thank you for being a part of my journey.

ACKNOWLEDGEMENTS

It's been over nine years since I started writing this book. It was after the loss of Scotty, my brother, that I made the decision to write my story. Scotty always said to me, "Little sister, you can do it!" in regard to just about everything from being a young mom, trying to attend college, and considering starting my first company. I know he would have said the same in regard to writing this book.

First and foremost, my two sons have been the loves of my life. It has been my two sons, Zack and Trey, who helped me realize what unconditional love is. It was my love for them that helped me to not give up, especially in regard to earning a college education. You help me want to be a better mom and person altogether. I am proud of each of you and love you very much.

My father's dream was to connect with his family again someday. I'm glad that after twenty-seven years of being apart, his dream came true. I'm glad to have met you nine years ago, and to have you in my life today.

Thank you to my good friend, Jim Buford, for all the encouragement, and for attending that first writing class with me in 2004 to help get me started on this book. Thank you to Harold Zallen, Embry Burrus, Stretch Dunn, Jerry Kelley, Terry Henley, Char Warren, James and Gloria Owens, and Gary Fuller for their reviews and encouragement over the past few years. Thank you to Thom Gossom, Jr., who has served as a special advisor to me in regard to this book and a friend. Thank you to my dearest friends: Andrea Musso, Sherry Shay, Don & Sandra Wilder (a.k.a. Dirty Don & Skanky Sandra), Bob Sanders, Beth Callahan Snipes, Toby & Char Warren, and the Tadych Family.

I would like to especially thank my friend and colleague, Dale Downing, who has been both my left and right hands through so much over the years. If I had to describe Dale with one word, it would be "loyal." Dale, I couldn't have done everything, including this book, without you. I am forever grateful to you for all the years of support. I love and appreciate you so much!

I thank my main editor, Carolyn Goss (www.Goodeditors.com), for helping with the start of this book several years ago and finally helping to wrap it up. I thank two contributing editors, Marian Carcache and Dean Bonner. Thank you, Amber Dickson, for your help doing research, public relations, and marketing of this book. Thank you to Robert Smith of www.flipflopfoto.com for the cover pictures. Also, thank you, John McNutt of McNutt & Company, LLC (www.leadershipbycreativity.com) for your professional layout and design services.

I'd like to make a special note to the members of the Auburn Football Lettermen Club, who I served as their club coordinator 2004 through 2013. I enjoyed being a part of the way you care and love each other, and reach out in special ways to your teammates and other members, especially during times of need. There's something very special about you guys that once played football for your beloved Auburn University. Some things in life are destined, and feeling I was a part of your family helped me. I could have never imagined feeling so loved and cared about by a more amazing group of people, and I thank you for the past nine years of your love during my tenure and since.

Thank you.

WITH SOME OF MY FRIENDS.

With Toby and Char Warren.

With Don Wilder, "Dirty Don." The only person missing from this picture is Skanky Sandra.

With Andrea Musso. If I listened to what others said… we would never have become friends.

Made in the USA
Charleston, SC
21 July 2013